PENGUIN BOOKS

WHAT MILLENNIALS WANT

Vivan Marwaha works on technology projects in emerging markets. A millennial himself, he cares deeply about understanding India and its future through its youth. He has lived and worked in New Delhi, Los Angeles and Washington D.C., and has written for the *Washington Post*, *New Statesman*, *Mint* and *Times of India*, among other publications. In 2022, he was featured in *Forbes* Asia's 30 Under 30 list.

PRAISE FOR THE BOOK

'*What Millennials Want* is an interesting and engaging perspective on Indian millennials. Vivan Marwaha takes a magnifying glass to the aspirations and challenges of young Indians in towns and cities, documenting their place in India's future. The future the millennials hope to build.' —Aaditya Thackeray

'Generous in detail and impeccably researched, Vivan's book *What Millennials Want* should be the quintessential read to understand how to harness India's 'demographic dividend'. The engaging narrative takes you through inner and outer landscapes of what Indian millennials think and feel, with many surprising insights. Vivan plays both scholarly guide and amiable travel companion with pleasing results. This book not only offers an enlightened view of this generation but prescriptive solutions for Indian millennials' unmet aspirations and lost opportunities which can only come from an author's passion for his contradictory subjects and for the contradictory nature of India.'—Lisa Ray

'Vivan Marwaha has written a compelling, detailed and intimate biography of the young Indians who will define India's future. A fascinating look into one of the world's largest groups of people—Indian millennials—this book is a must read for all those interested in the economic destiny of India, Asia and perhaps the world.'—Sanjeev Bikhchandani, Founder of naukri.com

'*What Millennials Want* is a timely and urgent work of scholarship. Taking us on a journey across the length and breadth of India, approaching young Indian life through a variety of lenses, Vivan Marwaha takes a bold step toward decoding the dreams and fears of what he terms "the largest generation in the world". Eminently readable and utterly fascinating.' —Dr Shashi Tharoor

'*What Millennials Want* is a surprisingly pessimistic reminder of how little India has changed.'—The Hindu BusinessLine

'*What Millennials Want* focuses on talking to people and decoding the problems of the generation through first-hand discussions.' —*Hindustan Times*

'According to Vivan Marwaha's book—*What Millennials Want*—this generation holds the key to the country's technological, economic and political future. Yet, we know surprisingly little about this key demographic.'—*GQ*

WHAT *millennials* WANT

Decoding the World's Largest Generation

VIVAN MARWAHA

PENGUIN BOOKS

An imprint of Penguin Random House

PENGUIN BOOKS

USA | Canada | UK | Ireland | Australia
New Zealand | India | South Africa | China

Penguin Books is part of the Penguin Random House group of companies
whose addresses can be found at global.penguinrandomhouse.com

Published by Penguin Random House India Pvt. Ltd
4th Floor, Capital Tower 1, MG Road,
Gurugram 122 002, Haryana, India

First published in Viking by Penguin Random House India 2021
Published in paperback by Penguin Books 2022

ISBN 9780143460084

For sale in the Indian Subcontinent only

Typeset in Adobe Caslon Pro by Manipal Technologies Limited, Manipal

www.penguin.co.in

To my grandparents

CONTENTS

INTRODUCTION

It was November 2018 in Jabalpur, Madhya Pradesh. I was at the city's famous Russel Chowk, talking to young people gathered here in the evening. Cars were honking and young men in bright polyester shirts with elaborately coiffed hair and multicoloured sunglasses were racing each other on their two-wheelers. The air, quickly cooling down, smelled of diesel and dust.

The market could have been called 'Chinese' or 'Electronics Chowk,' given how nearly every storefront was branded by two Chinese smartphone companies, Vivo and Oppo. One store was different. It was the only shop with people inside: Patanjali. A big outlet, it sold everything *swadeshi*, from cow ghee to fairness creams.

I was there to conduct interviews about the state assembly elections, where a high-pitched campaign between the Bharatiya Janata Party (BJP) and the Congress was coming to a close. Both parties were aggressively chasing millennial voters, luring them with promises of a million new jobs, unemployment allowances and even a lump sum of money at the time of marriage.[1]

As I was in the car on my way home, there were two kinds of advertisements on the radio. One encouraged voters to press on the lotus in the ongoing elections, and the other promoted a seemingly endless list of features of a Chinese smartphone.

There's a reason I was seeing and hearing all of this: those young people—Indian millennials—are a key to the success of the future of both technology and democracy in India. *They are the future of India.*

The companies and parties knew that and knew how important it was to target these millennials, even if millennials themselves didn't. I was in the market for a similar reason: If you want to understand the precipice that India is at and where it might go from here, you have to understand its millennials.

Born between 1981 and 1996, roughly numbering more than 440 million, they are, without any doubt, the largest millennial cohort on the planet.

~

Like every other generation in India, millennials are incredibly diverse: with not just significant economic division, but also important linguistic, regional, caste, gender and religious differences, which make the generation difficult to understand as a cohesive group.

Yet millennials have the potential to be India's most significant generation. If you're not convinced about why they could become the country's most important—and potentially most disruptive—generation, consider some of these numbers.

India's median age, according to a 2021 estimate by the CIA World Factbook, is twenty-eight years.[2] This means that half of its population is under the age of twenty-eight. By contrast, the median age in the world's top three economies—

namely, the United States, China, and Japan—is thirty-eight, thirty-seven and forty-seven years respectively. Among the top ten economies in the world, India has the youngest population followed distantly by Brazil, which has a median age of thirty-two years. By 2021, two-thirds of India's population will be within the working age of twenty to thirty-five years.[3]

These young Indians will be the world's largest labour force and market for goods and services. This is what is referred to as India's 'demographic dividend'. This term was popularized by academics, journalists, and businesspersons keen on investing in India in the early 2000s, who saw the country's youth as an asset in the longer-run, particularly when compared to China, a country whose one-child policy was viewed as a demographic crisis in the making. It was believed that with the right education and investment in human capital, a growing middle class, and an increase in foreign investment in the economy, India would not only enjoy high single-digit and even double-digit GDP growth, but its millennials and working-age population would power the country to transform itself like many east Asian success stories.

But are our millennials, the country's demographic dividend, paying out for the country the way we hoped? The rapid pace of technological change, the COVID-19 pandemic, the recent economic slowdown and accompanying effects of social pressure have the potential to create an alternate and divided future.

Demographic Dividend?

India's demographic dividend has similar odds of descending into a demographic disaster, mainly due to the poor quality of education which plagues most of the country's schools and universities. Largely built in haste to accommodate an exploding population, they are outdated institutions still using textbooks written decades ago. Furthermore, recent years of 'jobless growth' and low levels of job creation have kept millions unemployed. Unless the millions of India's young in its cities and countryside have well-paying jobs to provide them with financial stability and buying power, their potential will not be realized.

Along with the decline in economic opportunity, the increasing frequency of hate crimes and support for some long-standing projects of the Rashtriya Swayamsevak Sangh (RSS) have contributed to a sense that the country is moving towards majoritarianism. Many young people have been at the forefront of horrific incidents of gender, caste and communal violence in the country, and survey data confirm that support for authoritarianism has been steadily increasing with time.[4]

As India's economic liberalization was more focused on the formal sector of the economy, the informal and non-corporate sectors—where a majority of India's youth find their employment—continue to remain shackled. As a corollary, the share of informal workers in the Indian economy has only increased since liberalization, and millions continue to apply for low-level government jobs, simply because they are stable. This is why stories such as those reported by *The Washington Post*—about 19 million Indians applying for a mere 63,000 jobs in the railways, for instance—are surprising to foreign readers but unfortunately familiar to those acquainted with the Indian economy.[5]

India cannot hope to become a five or ten trillion-dollar economy if its youth spend their time either hunting for a low-paying government job or an activity so widespread as to earn its own academic term: timepass, when largely unemployed young men pass their time playing games and hanging out with friends.[6] Equally worrying are data which find that the number of women participating in paid work has been declining constantly since 2000. A World Bank study found that nearly 20 million women dropped out of the workforce between 2004 and 2012, and a Tata Sons-Dalberg analysis estimated that approximately 120 million women in India have a secondary education but do not participate in the workforce.[7]

India's millennials can only become a global power if they have cash in their wallets and stable jobs.

But there's scant attention paid to millennials as a unique generation. Instead of viewing them as independent islands of young Indians based on their caste, class, or religion, I hope to shine light on what brings them together—their common aspirations, anxieties, and experiences. When new policies and cultural issues are debated in India, lawmakers, news reporters and commentators all too often neglect to consider the impact these developments have on the millions of young Indians currently getting their education or joining the economy. The quality of their education; their opinions on hot-button cultural issues; their political beliefs; and whether they find employment will be crucial to India's future in the economic and political order of the 21st Century. As the country seeks to become a global leader, members of its most populous generation will soon become its most powerful, and it is hard to overstate the importance of understanding the attitudes, behaviours, and views of India's millennials.

It is largely understood that millennials in the West tend to skew more liberal on social issues than their predecessors. In 2017, 59 per cent of American millennials were registered as Democrats, while just 32 per cent were Republicans.[8] We know how these millennials think, and politicians, corporations and governments are now obsessed with tailoring their strategies to best speak to them. While we are gathering similar data in India, we are not close to understanding its millennials with the keen attention and nuance they deserve.

Defining Millennials

The term 'millennial' is often thrown around casually. I have spoken to countless parents and employers in Delhi, Mumbai and Bangalore, fed up with their millennial children or employees. They think this is an entitled, spoiled generation addicted to social media and instant gratification. I will present evidence to challenge this popular opinion across the pages of this book.

But who exactly is a millennial?

The Pew Research Center, a renowned American polling and surveying 'fact tank', defines millennials as those born between 1981 and 1996.[9] While generational definitions are clearly not an exact science, Pew believes that the people born in this timespan have a set of shared experiences which animate their views and shape their attitudes. For example, millennials in the United States were between the ages of five and twenty during the 9/11 attacks which altered the country and its people forever.

In the Indian context, and for the purposes of my book, I also find the 1981–1996 cut-off helpful. Not because of 9/11, but the 1991 economic liberalization, which is believed to have significantly changed the nature of work and life in India. The oldest millennials were nine during liberalization, and the youngest were yet to be born. But they have all had similar experiences of witnessing India 'transform' before their eyes.

Some may question the wisdom of defining Indian millennials as those born between these years. But India did not become fully capitalist even by 1996. The opening of the country's economy in 1991 didn't mean that its socialist institutions evaporated overnight. Foreign investment took years to trickle in, and economic growth only started taking off in the latter half of the nineties. Furthermore, the effects of liberalization were initially only felt by urban elites, who were best positioned to take advantage of more open markets. The rest of India had a different experience. Rural poverty remained largely unchanged, and rising discontent across the country led to the defeat of the incumbent Congress government in 1996.

When I describe my research to people, I often get asked what other generations are called. I was scrolling through Twitter one morning when I came across an interesting tweet by journalist and political commentator, Nitin Pai,[10] who divided the generations in India in an insightful manner:

- 'Midnight's Children' for those born between 1935 and 1955.
- 'Gen AIR', referring to All India Radio, for those born between 1956 and 1975.
- 'Gen DD', referring to Doordarshan for those born between 1976 and 1996.
- 'Reform Brats' for those born between 1996 and 2005.
- 'Hashtag Brats' for those born on and after 2006.

It isn't hard to see the logic here. Midnight's Children were most shaped by India's independence, which occurred on the midnight of 15 August 1947. Millions in the northern and eastern regions of the Indian subcontinent had either migrated to India or seen their communities entirely displaced. Gen AIR refers to the children of socialism. Cities were just beginning to expand, job options were limited, and most of India still lived in its villages. The Congress Party essentially controlled all political power and maintained a socialist command over the economy. Only those in big cities with high incomes and electricity connections owned televisions, and All India Radio was the primary source of news and music. This era saw bank nationalization, the Emergency and two wars with Pakistan. It also saw simmering anger and discontent. *Garibi Hatao* became the cause of the country as privy purses were abolished and the state undertook far-reaching measures to redistribute wealth. Amitabh Bachchan's iconic 'Angry Young Man' persona in *Deewar* perhaps best represented youth sentiment of the time. In its subversiveness, the film, and Bachchan's character Vijay, reflected the simmering anti-establishment mood in the country. Protests were breaking out, and Indira Gandhi would soon impose Emergency, curtailing democracy and fundamental rights for two years.

Pai's Doordarshan generation spans the millennials' era—though of course the former precedes the latter by several years. But this was the time when Doordarshan diversified from providing news to entertainment. *Hum Log*, the first sponsored show on Indian television, explored the aspirations and challenges of a middle-class Indian family. Its episodes averaged fifty million viewers, resonating strongly with the country's urban and young populations. Shah Rukh Khan vaulted into the public domain with his role as a soldier in *Fauji*. This is when India's millennials were born. A time of opportunity and hope. The economy would soon open itself to the outside world, and jobs in new sunrise industries began to offer alternatives to medicine and the public sector.

Older millennials were in school during liberalization, and they joined the workforce nine years later, in 2000, when the effects of capitalism were beginning to take hold. Younger millennials joined the workforce a few years later.

This book relies on a wealth of data to investigate Indian millennials. There are two principal sources I used to make my observations and illustrate trends. One was a study conducted in April and May 2016 by the Center for the Study in Developing Societies (CSDS) along with the Konrad Adenaeur Stitfung (KAS), hereafter referred to as the 'CSDS study'. The CSDS study was conducted in nineteen states, with 6122 respondents in the age group of fifteen to thirty-four years. This implies that some individuals younger than millennials have been sampled in the survey, but given the study is the best source of data on Indian youth, the benefits of using the findings of the study for a book on millennials outweigh the possible drawbacks of including non-millennials. The survey was conducted using a standardized questionnaire and was translated into the local language whenever necessary. As I was examining sources of data for the book, I found that the CSDS study stood out in its data collection, which was conducted manually, and used different languages, which implies that the respondents did not all speak the same language or hail from similar backgrounds. Since the CSDS survey placed a preference on urban youth (which the authors believed would allow them 'a deeper analysis of youth living in different types of urban areas—both big and small'), the scholars weighted the sample 'in a manner that it mirrors the actual rural-urban profile of India's 15-34-year-old population as per Census 2011 data'.[11]

In addition to quantitative research, this book relies heavily on qualitative fieldwork, mainly in-person interviews I conducted with more than 900 millennials, educators, business leaders, politicians, and policymakers across thirteen Indian states in order to investigate the trends discovered in the CSDS study. In these states, which were almost equally divided between the four geographical regions of India, I travelled to villages, towns and cities to best investigate some of the trends which define millennials. Some of these interviews were long conversations, where I met my subjects over multiple visits, while others were shorter five to twenty-five-minute interactions which took place wherever I found millennials willing to talk to me. These were across a wide variety of public spaces—from food stalls at crowded marketplaces to parking lots near coaching centres. For some of the individuals profiled in this book, I have changed names or identifying details. These were made at the request of my respondents, to protect their privacy.

Others might take a narrower approach to looking at millennials, focusing on certain people or issues more commonly associated with the generation today, but this book takes a broader view, piecing together diverse trends, events, and experiences to provide a roadmap to understanding their aspirations and anxieties.

EDUCATION

In 1961, the government of Prime Minister Jawaharlal Nehru established two Indian Institutes of Management (IIMs), the first in Calcutta and the second in Ahmedabad. Calcutta was established in conjunction with the Massachusetts Institute of Technology's Sloan School of Management, while the campus in Ahmedabad was to collaborate with the Harvard Business School.

The institutions, which have trained some of India's and the world's brightest business leaders, were the product of an inherently socialist idea. Almost ten years after independence from British colonial rule, there were simply not enough managers for India's numerous public sector enterprises. These public undertakings, from mining corporations to ordnance factories, required well-trained executives to steer the young country's industrial growth, and native talent was in short supply. The Planning Commission of India, the Soviet-inspired body which was tasked with developing five-year plans for the growth of the Indian economy, invited Professor George Robbins from the University of California, Los Angeles, to fix this problem and help conceive an education institution to offer young Indians a practical business education.

Since then, investments were made in expanding university education, and the two institutions soon grew to twenty. The flagship institutions boast of a roster of hugely successful alumni, from RBI governor Raghuram Rajan and cricket commentator Harsha Bhogle to novelist Chetan Bhagat and former PepsiCo worldwide CEO Indira Nooyi, among numerous others in the Indian and global financial system. But they just weren't enough. As Indians began to see these elite institutions as a ticket to a prosperous job at a multinational, and eventually, a career outside India, admission became extremely competitive. The private sector began to fill the gap between the demand and supply, and since then, thousands of private colleges opened across India to offer students a management education.

Most of India's education system has a similar story. Today, the few good universities, colleges and schools, largely founded by the government or built during colonial rule, educate only a small number of individuals, while a vast private sector has mushroomed to fill the gaps in what the government failed to universalize.

What all of this has created is a deeply flawed system which tends to reward those with existing privileges or resources. Karthik Muralidharan, the Tata Chancellor's Professor of economics at the University of California, San Diego, finds that the Indian education system is not built to educate students, but to filter them.[1] In a 2005 paper, with co-authors Gretchen Cheney and Betsy Ruzzi, he argues that historically education in India served as a 'gatekeeper, permitting an avenue of upward mobility only to those with resources'.[2] Unfortunately, this remains true in 2021. Indian students spend years studying for board examinations, college entrance examinations, and public sector job tests to continuously filter them towards better opportunities. But in all the rote memorization and formulae required for success, the most significant purpose of learning—education, gets lost.

Although the privatization taking place in the sector was intended to make it more inclusive, it was, in fact, exclusionary and insufficient. Furthermore, India's early prioritization of tertiary education came at the expense of primary-level schooling, creating vast inequities and poor standards of education that continue to this very day. These problems only exacerbated as India's population continued to increase, as socialist India could not provide employment to the millions of young Indians who needed it. As the economy began to open up, the growth of Information Technology services in the country led to the creation of coaching industries dedicated to preparing students to either become software engineers or government servants. This is not because the education system had succeeded in preparing students for the future, but rather because it had failed.

In effect, India created an elaborate system which serves to filter its students towards IITs, IIMs and public service jobs instead of educating them to succeed in the modern economy.

Millennials have largely finished their education at the time of writing this book, and their time in school or college is not the first experience we may think about when understanding the generation. But if we're looking at many of the challenges millennials face today, it's because of the education system.

•————•

Rocket Singh

It was a humid day in South Mumbai in May 2018 when I found my Uber driver after fifteen minutes of back-and-forth on the phone. Traffic had backed up at the Gateway of India as I was leaving Colaba to make a lunch meeting in Parel. The map showed a thirty-five-minute journey, and as we began driving, I knew I'd be late.

I didn't care. I could have stayed in that cab for hours.

I've had some pretty interesting conversations with Uber, Lyft, Grab and other taxi drivers around the world. From a driver advocating for the imposition of Sharia law in California to another ranting about how female passengers made life difficult for drivers in Hyderabad, I thought I had heard it all.

Until I met Ravindra.

Ravindra was a 27-year-old migrant to Mumbai. Originally from Hazaribagh in Jharkhand, Ravindra loved his life in the Maximum City. He had worked in Delhi for a few years, but he found the heat a deal-breaker. I heard this in amazement as I wiped the sweat trickling down my forehead despite being in an oppressively air-conditioned vehicle.

As we drove past the Chhatrapati Shivaji Terminus, I asked a friend who was in the car with me, whether it was the same as the Victoria Terminus, Mumbai's gothic railway station built in the global jubilee of Queen Victoria's reign.

Registering my curiosity, Ravindra told me that the Chhatrapati Shivaji Terminus and Victoria Terminus were indeed the same building. I appreciated his interjection, and we got talking about Mumbai, its weather, and his business as an Uber driver. The conversation soon took a sharp turn, and Ravindra began to speak about Muhammad Ali Jinnah, the founding father of Pakistan. In great detail, he told me how Mohandas Gandhi and Muhammad Ali Jinnah had conspired to break India into two separate countries. That Gandhi would rule Hindus in India, while Jinnah would control Muslims in Pakistan. What I found most interesting was how he kept referring to Jinnah as female. I decided silence was my best strategy in this 'conversation', so I let him continue without interruption. I soon discovered that he believed that Jinnah was Gandhi's wife (yes, I'm not making this up), and that Gandhi had decided to install Jinnah in Pakistan after dividing the Indian subcontinent. I stayed completely silent until I broke it to him that Jinnah was in fact, a man, not even remotely related to Gandhi—certainly not his wife.

I don't think my comments registered, because he soon pivoted the conversation to Indira Gandhi—who he thought was the Mahatma's daughter—telling me how she and Sonia Gandhi had looted all of India's riches to send them to Italy. He was following the same thread of conversation—Mahatma Gandhi wanted to 'rule' India, so his supposed descendants were trying to carry forward this plan. It was pretty fascinating to hear in-person conspiracy theories normally espoused online by right-wing activists and trolls. At this point, I could no longer stay silent. I interrupted him and asked where he got this information from.

WhatsApp.

This wasn't a surprise to me. I was well aware that WhatsApp, the instant messaging mobile application that had become wildly successful in India on the back of the country's smartphone boom, also served as India's largest unofficial fake news service and encyclopaedia for 'facts' circulated by nefarious organizations. With more than 400 million active monthly users in 2019, it's not an exaggeration to say WhatsApp connects India.[3] Apart from the daily 'good morning' greetings, photos of babies smiling, and pictures of different deities superimposed with spiritual messages sent by millions of Indians on WhatsApp every day, the application also has a dangerous underbelly: It has become an incubator for conspiracies, fake news, and most dangerously, mob violence.

On a particularly chilling day in 2017, seven men were killed in two separate incidents in Ravindra's home state of Jharkhand. Uttam Verma, a survivor of one of the Jharkhand mob attacks recounted his experience to *The New York Times*, telling the newspaper that a group of villagers had stopped him and his brother, accusing them of being child stealers.[4] When the brothers couldn't produce their identification cards, the group began attacking them with bricks, sticks and swords. Soon, the crowd swelled to almost 500 and killed Uttam's brother and two friends who came to help them out. In a state where human trafficking claims its biggest toll—with thousands of young boys and girls abducted every year and trafficked to India's cities to work as domestic servants and labourers—child abduction is a particularly sensitive issue. Animesh Naithany, the deputy policy superintendent of Jharkhand, told the *Times* that 'rumours of children being abducted spread on WhatsApp like wildfire. Villagers started keeping vigil around their villages. Since they are an illiterate lot, they cannot differentiate between a real piece of news and a rumour.'

But I digress. This is about Ravindra.

He was one of the fortunate ones. He finished all twelve grades of school in Hazaribagh and went to join one of his brothers who worked in Jordan as a fabric cutter, but he quit his job after six months and returned to India. He found the Arab heat oppressive, and based on our conversations, I also sensed a certain level of animosity towards Islam. His father stopped talking to him for six months after he quit, enraged that his son had given up a well-paying job to return to India. Ravindra's family couldn't understand why he had done such a thing.

Until he started driving for Uber.

Ravindra applied for a commercial driving license and used the part of his savings that he hadn't sent to his parents to take out a loan to buy a Suzuki Swift D'Zire. He signed up for both Uber and Ola and began driving in Mumbai. While some days weren't as good as others, Ravindra was making between Rs 32,000 and Rs 38,000 a month. He lived in a small flat in Nalasopara, thirty-five kilometres from Mumbai, and most of his trips were from South Mumbai to Bandra, ferrying some of India's highest earning professionals from home to work and work to home.

When I first met Ravindra, he loved driving for Uber. Since he could set his own schedule, he chose to drive from 6 a.m. to 11 a.m., and then again from 4 p.m. to 9 p.m., taking advantage of surge pricing during peak office traffic. He couldn't have asked for a better job. Unlike many Uber drivers in India who drive as a full-time job, Ravindra had loftier ambitions of using the gig as a bridge to a better life.

He spent his spare afternoons time taking computer lessons. He wanted a desk job. When asked what this job would entail, Ravindra didn't have an answer. He simply wanted a job at a desk, with a computer in front of him, like the one Ranbir Kapoor had in his film, *Rocket Singh: Salesman of the Year*. In the film, Kapoor plays an honest salesman who refuses to offer kickbacks to clients to land their contracts. It celebrates Rocket Singh's honesty in standing up for his values instead of capitulating to his company and helping carry out its shady dealings.

That wasn't Ravindra's plan, though. He told me he would wholeheartedly offer his clients bribes and kickbacks, since that's how things get done in India. He went on to criticize Rocket Singh for having his head in the wrong place. Needless to say, I found this pretty fascinating. He had based his life choices on a Bollywood film but wanted to do the opposite of what the film's protagonist did.

He was most excited about a desk job because, growing up, it was seen as the ultimate sign of having made it. Only government officers had desk jobs where Ravindra grew up, and so he wanted one too. He, too, wanted to make a stable salary, insulated by the unpredictable nature of rural work or driving for an app, and buy a house for himself and his new family.

But when I met Ravindra a few months later in December 2018, something had changed. He now hated his life. He had realized that he could never achieve the life he wanted: that of his passengers. He didn't want to grow old driving people his age around. He wanted more. He wanted *their* life.

Ravindra tried everything to get a desk job somewhere. After taking computer lessons, he created a profile on Naukri.com, India's homegrown version of LinkedIn; paid an acquaintance to help him write a CV; and even bought some collared shirts for interviews.

The interviews never came. Ravindra didn't hear back from a single place to which he applied. While he didn't know how to code, he thought he could manage accounts or enter data at a shop or small business. He didn't realize that he needed accounting experience for such roles and an established network to get his foot in the door. Too many jobs, it seemed, were reserved for those who had existing relationships with someone at these companies and enterprises.

Ravindra is not alone. This is the story of millions of India's millennials. They grew up in small towns but possess big-city aspirations. Facebook, WhatsApp, YouTube and Google have brought the world to their fingertips. They know how others live, but they don't necessarily feel empowered or know how to get there.

Ravindra went to a private Hindi-medium school in Hazaribagh. His parents chose to send him and his brothers to a private school because it had bathrooms and was close to their home. Its tuition was roughly Rs 500 a month, which wasn't a huge expense for his father who owned a cycle repair shop in town. Ravindra wasn't a good or a bad student. He was average. He never failed his exams, but he didn't excel at anything either.

For his final two years of school, he chose the only stream, or combination of subjects his school offered: science. He took physics, chemistry, mathematics, biology and Hindi, to fulfil his parents' hopes of making each of their sons engineers. The biggest nightmare for Indian students, the infamous class twelve board exam, also went reasonably well for Ravindra. His average was 54 per cent, which was in line with his peers, but by no means was it a score that would help him become a successful engineer.

With that, Ravindra told me, he had a ceiling put on his life. Born to an upper-caste family, he could not make use of India's reservations to secure a spot at a good college or university. He would have to compete in the general category, with children from more affluent families who could afford better schools or tuition centres to help them succeed.

Ravindra did not have many options. He could have enrolled in a government engineering college in Jharkhand, but he knew some people who had attended those and were still unemployed. His family income and scores were too low for him to gain admission into the Ranchi outpost of the prestigious Birla Institute of Technology and Science, a private alternative to the Indian Institute of Technology (IIT) system. Vocational and job-training programmes to help him become a computer programmer or mining engineer weren't good quality, and friends of his who went through these programmes continued to remain unemployed. This was when he decided to skip getting a university education and went to Jordan to join his brother, who worked as a fabric cutter there. He was making almost Rs 30,000 a month and saving most of it, which he sent back home to his parents. He lived with his brother in a one-room apartment, which he showed me on his phone. It looked comfortable and spacious, a refreshing change from the poor living conditions many Indian migrant labourers are forced into while working elsewhere in the Middle East.

Ravindra thought Jordan would be like Dubai, a desert metropolis which has become a favoured vacation destination for middle class Indian families. But Amman and Dubai have very little in common. Almost 50 per cent Indian, Dubai can often feel like an extension of India, particularly Bur Dubai, a predominantly Indian neighbourhood with the only Hindu temple in the entire United Arab Emirates. Its glitzy skyscrapers and family-friendly amusement parks are major attractions to families from small-town India. Four-day packaged tours with flights, hotel accommodation and a desert safari can be purchased starting at Rs 30,000. Ravindra left middle India for the Middle East expecting the glitz and the glamour of Dubai.

Amman, also a melting-pot of nationalities and cultures has an entirely different character. Amman, too, has a diverse population, but only a fraction of Dubai's Indians—its diversity comes largely from its population of Syrian and Palestinian refugees. Ravindra knew nothing about the delicate politics of the Middle East before landing in Jordan. He didn't need to either, given his roommate was his brother, and his supervisor a Pakistani from Sindh. Before reaching Amman, Ravindra thought he'd be able to freely access alcohol and find a girlfriend. He was disappointed. He couldn't find single Hindu girls to date and while alcohol was available, he had no friends to party with.

'Jordan was nothing like India. I was working all the time and I couldn't do anything there,' he told me. 'I felt trapped in a cage.'

Although Ravindra knew fabric cutting wasn't the most exciting job available, the prospect of adventure and the thrill of discovering a new country excited him. He wanted to be anonymous, and in Amman, nobody knew him.

However, the life he had dreamt he would be leading in Jordan remained just a dream. With long working hours and a culture he failed to understand or appreciate, Ravindra felt alone. He lacked friends and began to lose motivation. He soon decided to move back home to India, where 'achhe din' had just begun. He thought he would use his savings to start his own life, make more money and settle down.

Moving back was much harder than he anticipated. He tried looking for fabric cutting jobs in Delhi, but he wasn't able to find anything. He eventually got work as a security guard in a South Delhi home but couldn't adjust to the harsh demands of his night shift. He then moved to Mumbai, where another of his other brothers was a supervisor at a construction site, but Ravindra was not attracted to the low pay or the physical demands of a construction worker's job. He then started driving for Uber, which is when I met him for the first time and had my fascinating discussion on Gandhi, Jinnah and their secret relationship.

The second time I met Ravindra, he had realized his professional life had hit a wall. Without a formal university education, there was not much he could do. Driving for Uber was one of the few opportunities to maintain a decent and stable income. But it also showed him every day how his life was different from the lives of his passengers. No matter how hard he tried, he couldn't switch places with them.

The dreams he had fostered and nourished outside India all decayed quickly when he returned, and he realized that his education had not prepared him to break into the life he aspired.

Ravindra's story isn't unique. Millions of young Indians have similar experiences. Here's why.

~

Translating Schooling into Learning

India's education problems begin at the very bottom of the system: primary schools. The percentage of children enrolled in schools is higher than ever before, having steadily increased in the last two decades in large part due to government initiatives and interventions such as the Right to Education (RTE) Act and the Mid Day Meal Scheme. However, the quality of education is failing them.

The findings of the 2017 Annual Status of Education Report (ASER), released by Pratham, one of India's largest education-focused NGOs, were deeply worrying. The report, titled 'Beyond Basics', which focused on abilities most young Indians should possess before they reach adulthood, revealed a massive deficit of basic reading, arithmetic and functional skills among India's youth.

The ASER team surveyed more than 30,000 fourteen-to-eighteen-year-olds in twenty-eight districts across twenty-four states. One of its most stark revelations was that almost 25 per cent of respondents failed to read basic text fluently in their native language.[5] Think about that for a second. A quarter of those enrolled in school, aged fourteen to eighteen, cannot read their own language at a basic level. Sixty per cent, or less than two-thirds of the eighteen-year-olds surveyed could read English sentences, and of that group, 79 per cent knew the meaning of those sentences. This means that 40 per cent of eighteen-year-olds could not read English, a language of increasing importance in the modern economy, and over 20 per cent of those who could read English failed to comprehend the meaning of what they read.

The problems aren't limited to reading. Over half of those fourteen to eighteen-year-olds surveyed struggled with basic division. Pratham asked them to perform a problem: dividing a three-digit number by a single digit number (dividing 872 by seven, for example). Only 43 per cent could successfully perform this. ASER tests the ability to do basic division as an indicator of their proficiency in arithmetic. It goes without saying that students' inability to conduct even basic arithmetic operations at such a late age points to a massive failing of the Indian education system, of the kind that can truly hinder their future academic and professional success. Perhaps even more concerning among the report's findings was that the proportion of the youth who have not acquired basic math skills at age fourteen is almost the same as that of those aged eighteen, indicating that the four years of secondary schooling does not create any additional learning or academic development among students. As the report highlights, 'learning deficits seen in elementary school in previous years seem to carry forward as young people go from being adolescents to young adults'.[6]

To see the evidence behind this data, I visited a few different government schools in Delhi, Haryana and Bihar.

Bihar is often called India's 'basket case' due to its abysmal performance on economic and human development indices. It is a land of fertile soil and ancient culture and a melting pot of an array of religious and caste groups. Long considered India's Wild West, the state was, for many decades, a hotbed for gang rivalry and feudal politics, a place which saw a significant breakdown of governance and law enforcement. In recent years, the state has begun to stage a comeback. In 2005, the election of the reform-minded Nitish Kumar resulted in new government initiatives to fix the education system, improve law and order, and create economic growth. In an important step to improve enrolment in schools, girls were given bicycles to make it easier for them to go to school. However, there is a long way to go.

Education in Bihar is one of the domains where the state continues to fail. In a piece appropriately titled 'School Education in Bihar has Collapsed,' *The Hindu* newspaper reported that almost two-thirds (64 per cent) of the 1.2 million students who took their class twelve board exams in Bihar in 2017, had failed.[7] And of the few who did pass, only 8 per cent scored over 60 per cent. The class twelve board exam is arguably the most important school examination that Indian children take. Often the only criterion for college admission, the Indian board examination system has come under constant fire for its flaws and the pressure it puts on students. Nevertheless, it remains a crucial milestone that students must cross.

For years, if not decades, the board examination in Bihar was something of a running joke. Cheating was almost universal, and in many instances, teachers and invigilators would either leak papers ahead of time or hand out the answers in the examination halls. After efforts to curb this elaborate and growing 'cheating industry,' cheating has gone down, but failure rates have shot up.

I decided to go beyond the headlines and spend a few days at some of these schools in the greater Patna region. I went in early 2018, but it often felt like it could have been 1988 or even 1958. These schools, which I was told were fairly new, felt like they had been built decades ago to educate students in an era where computers did not exist.

Most of the schools I visited were single-storey structures, all painted baby pink. One of the schools, which supposedly had students from grade one through eight, only had two classrooms. Well, it had three, but the third was used as a kitchen to prepare midday meals. A simple math calculation would tell you that it was six classrooms short. I was confused as to where the other six classes were held. The answer was in plain sight: Teachers were holding classes in corridors, with students packed like sardines. Although the law prohibits government schools from turning children away, many teachers and administrators told me that the overcrowding had forced some schools to do so.

On paper, these schools are supposed to operate from about 9 a.m. to 4 p.m. In practice, they begin at about 10 a.m. and finish a little before 3 p.m., with a one-and-a-half-hour lunch break in between. That's about three-and-a-half hours of instruction daily. Because teachers' salaries are extremely low, schools fail to attract good instructors, and chronic short-staffing causes teachers to wear many hats: The math teacher often doubles or triples up to teach science or Hindi and may often also help in serving midday meals. On any given day, it is common for many teachers to not appear at work. They're either running their own errands or taking care of other personal business. Even if they do show up, they may not always teach. In my most memorable classroom visit, I saw a teacher sitting at the front, with a girl applying *mehendi* on her hands. The teacher later told me that she had a wedding to attend that day, which is why she got one of her students to apply her henna. I nodded, indicating I understood, acting as if this was totally normal.

At that time, the teacher seemed to be conducting a computer science lesson for her seventh graders. I know this not because there were any open computers or any bits of code written on the blackboard—in fact, the school didn't have any computers at all—but because of a series of 'True or False' statements on the blackboard.

"True/False:"

1. Computer can do calculations ( )
2. Computer stores information ( )
3. The word 'computer' is derived from the French word 'compute' ( )
4. Computer is just like a calculator ( )
5. A few years later you won't live without a computer ( )

Different students were being called up to the board to fill in the parentheses with their answers as the teacher watched over the proceedings, while continuing to have her *mehendi* applied. I couldn't help but think how the system was failing these kids. The fifth statement was particularly rich with irony. Computers are, in fact, integral to most human activity today. And yet, the only knowledge these children had of them was from a blackboard with five random factoids (four, since the first and fourth were essentially the same), including a statement on how essential the machines are.

Many classrooms didn't have proper furniture or fittings either. There were almost never more than a handful of desks, and fans were a luxury. I visited in February; I could not even imagine how harsh the condition would be in May or July. The schools all had a distinctive smell, of urine. Because many lacked bathrooms, children would urinate behind the building, staircases, or in any areas that offered relative privacy. Girls who were menstruating stayed home, due to the lack of sanitation facilities for them at school. Given that these schools were often used for public functions after hours, nothing could be left outside, or it would be stolen. One headmaster told me how taps, pipes and other water fittings were all stolen in the span of one night by local villagers.

This is not just about a set of schools I visited in Bihar. It's about an education system in India which, at every step of the way, sets its children up for failure. The elite academies of Delhi and Bombay—famous for educating the country's rich and powerful—are not the schools most young Indians attend. They attend government or inexpensive private schools in rural India and in tier-two or three cities. When the state fails to educate them, it fails them for the rest of their lives.

Indians place great value on education. As millions move from the farm to the city in search of better incomes and opportunities, they need a modern education to not just thrive but survive. Many of the kids surveyed by ASER were first-generation learners, expected to perform tasks that their uneducated parents or grandparents could not perform. However, they did not fare well on executing some of these tasks.[8] 76 per cent could count money correctly, 56 per cent could add weights accurately, and less than two-thirds (64 per cent) could successfully take financial decisions such as managing a budget or making a purchase. In terms of general knowledge, 79 per cent could name the state they lived in, and only 64 per cent knew the name of India's capital. It has become clear that while enrolment numbers are at an all-time high, schooling in India has unfortunately not translated into learning.

These numbers are not meant to inundate you with facts on how India's young are failing at basic literacy, math, and in performing daily tasks, but to highlight a systemic problem that is setting them up for continued disappointment and possible failure: the lack of good education. As the term 'demographic dividend' gets thrown around regularly in the media and academic circles with respect to India, it is important to seriously examine whether this dividend can be realized or the situation will descend into a demographic disaster. As young Indians join the workforce, they need strong foundations to succeed. India's schools do not provide this foundation. As the founder of Pratham, Madhav Chavan has written, 'It is already recognized that the skills required for today's jobs are not provided by yesterday's education even if we ignore the rather low level of abilities the young demonstrate.'[9] As the very meaning of work evolves at a rapid pace, India's youth are woefully ill-equipped to find a place not just in a rapidly shifting future, but even in the present economy.

India currently spends roughly 4 per cent of its GDP on education, a paltry sum for a developing country.[10] This has disastrous effects on the entire education system. Government schools cannot pay teachers good salaries and fail to attract competent, let alone good, talent. Hard infrastructure is neglected, and many schools lack basic facilities such as toilets, desks, fans, electricity, and even adequate classrooms. Ensuring sufficient school supplies or conducting remedial after-school workshops is usually out of the question. Although most millennials were done with school in the 2010s, low quality education has put this this generation on the backfoot for decades to come.

These challenges are only exacerbated as students mature. Most Indian universities, relics of the past, haven't had their curricula updated in decades. Due to low endowments and a lack of funding, not only do hiring and research suffer, but universities are unable to maintain good libraries, while basic facilities such as academic counselling and career services centres are non-existent. If parents have some money saved up, they prefer to send their children abroad—to Singapore,

Australia, England, Canada or the United States—so that they can get a better education and access better job opportunities.

In fact, data shared in the Indian Parliament by the Ministry of Human Resource Development, the government body charged with overseeing and managing the entire country's education systems, revealed that *more than half* of the central government's entire budget for higher education went to educate *just three per cent* of the country's students between 2015 and 2018.[11] These funds were allocated to the ninety-seven IITs, IIMs, National Institutes of Technology (NITs), and the Indian Institutes of Informational Technology (IIITs). The biggest recipients are the IITs, which receive almost 27 per cent of all higher education funding, but only educate 1.18 per cent of Indian college students. Meanwhile, 865 other public and private institutions which educate more than 97 per cent of the country's college students, have to fight for the remaining 48.9 per cent of funding. Although the data only revealed funding for 2015 to 2018, Pallam Raju, the former minister responsible for India's human resource development, confirmed that these skewed funding levels had been the norm for years.[12] Sukhadeo Thorat, former president of the University Grants Commission, criticized higher education funding for being 'hierarchical', and compared it to the caste system, faulting the government for funding certain institutions, while under-funding others. While IITs have had a successful track record in educating top quality Indian engineers, it is becoming clear that they are doing this at the expense of basically everyone else.

It is estimated that to be competitive in the global economy, India will need to build a thousand universities and 50,000 colleges to educate 100 million young people in the next decade.[13] And that's just to match supply with demand, without considering the quality of the degrees offered.

At the time of Independence, India had roughly twenty universities and fewer than 500 colleges across the country. Roughly seven decades later, there are now about 760 universities and more than 40,000 colleges, educating approximately 35 million students.[14,15] According to Prof. Devesh Kapur at Johns Hopkins University, since the year 2000, India has added 4.4 colleges per day, but as the quantity of education offered expanded at this unprecedented pace, quality plummeted.[16] Today, the chronic lack of well-trained faculty, severe shortage of academic resources such as reference books or laboratory facilities, and outdated curricula are putting shackles on the ambitions and abilities of current students and graduates. There are small towns and cities all across India where the only economic activity seems to come from the education industry. Education barons, often local politicians, have become dollar millionaires and multi-millionaires in these places, selling degrees like common commodities.[17] In many instances, they operate real estate rackets under the guise of private engineering colleges.[18] These political strongmen are able to line their pockets even as they blatantly fail their students. And this real estate and for-profit nexus has grave second order repercussions, since all private institutions are clubbed together by regulators. Therefore, any policy or regulation to attack malignant actors in the education sector unintentionally hamstrings even benevolent private institutions. A restriction on tuition, for instance, might be aimed at reining in private players, but also inhibits honest institutions from investing to improve the quality of their education.

In vast swathes of India, instead of seeing a robust manufacturing sector, it has become eerily clear that private colleges and coaching centres have become the real factories, churning out degrees of spurious quality.

For students to attain good quality education, massive investments in both hard and soft infrastructure are required. Education in India is a series of vicious cycles. Vast numbers of children don't have the resources or means to access quality primary education, which severely hampers their ability to progress at higher levels, even as the state fails to provide them with good education at those levels. The gaps widen every year, eventually rendering them unemployable or unskilled when they graduate. A 2016 survey of second year master students at a well-reputed state university in Maharashtra asked students six simple questions from a class six mathematics textbook. Only eleven out of 200 students could answer them correctly.[19] The India Skills Report, a 2018 survey of more than 500,000 college students across twenty-nine Indian states and seven union territories conducted by the Confederation of Indian Industries (CII), the All India Council of Technical Education (AICTE), the United Nations Development Fund, and two private consulting firms found that approximately half of engineering students surveyed and less than half of B-Pharma students were employable at the time of graduation.[20] The employability of other students, such as those enrolled in MBA or MCA programmes was even lower, at around 40 per cent. And only approximately a third of BCom and BA graduates were employable. These figures, while up around 35 per cent since 2014, are all truly appalling.

The CSDS study revealed that almost a third of India's youth lists 'student' as their current occupation, up 19 per cent from 2007. These young people are essentially moving from one degree to the next. After graduating from school, they attain an undergraduate education in any institution where their class twelve board exam results meet the cut-off requirements. Given the poor quality of higher education, public and private, and the lack of robust overall employment, they find it hard to get a job, so they decide to enrol in another degree.

A rise in rural incomes aided by a large expansion in government welfare schemes, an increase in the pressure on farm incomes, and the continued subdivision of rural holdings, led millions of millennials from agricultural families to attain higher education in hopes of finding careers away from farm work. Low quality government colleges and private institutions driven by profit are filling the demand and supply gap. But here is when these millennials encounter the other demand and supply problem: There are simply not enough jobs available to match their qualifications on paper, and even if those jobs did exist, the quality of their degrees would make them unemployable.

The India Skills Report is one of the more optimistic assessments on employability among Indian graduates.[21] A 2019 report conducted by the employability assessment firm Aspiring Minds found that 80 per cent of engineers are not employable for any job in the knowledge economy, a whopping 95 per cent of engineering graduates cannot even code, and only 2.5 per cent possess the required skills in Artificial Intelligence (AI) which the industry requires.[22] As India experienced its own dot-com bubble and technology boom in the late 1990s and 2000s, millions of young men and women chose to study engineering and computer science to join homegrown technology and outsourcing giants such as Infosys, Wipro or Tata Consultancy Services. To match the demand for engineers and computer scientists, thousands of private colleges opened across the country. Most of these were money-making institutions which failed or were not committed to providing a decent quality of education to their students. This led to a two-fold problem: a decline in available jobs as the supply of engineers and computer scientists increased, and a sharp rise in the number of insufficiently skilled and qualified graduates. This system has created a glut of graduates who are engineers in name only. The existing challenges of poor-quality education and old curricula have only intensified as the world moves towards the greater adoption of technology, machine learning and automation. Although the AICTE has started tightening its rules on issuing certificates to new colleges, the damage has been done.

~

A Booming T.I.M.E. for Indore

I was in Indore, the financial capital of Madhya Pradesh, in April 2019 during the Lok Sabha elections. It was the same month that Indore had just won its third consecutive award for being India's cleanest city. Its residents are proud to claim this distinction. And with good reason—the city truly stands apart in its cleanliness. Even in its crowded old town, home to a vibrant late-night food market, Sarafa Bazaar, it is hard to find trash or waste where it doesn't belong.

But driving around Indore, more than the visible cleanliness, I was struck by the hundreds, if not thousands, of coaching centres, colleges and finishing schools.

At first glance, Indore was truly booming. New shopping malls were opening, and people were flocking from all over India to the city.

But as students.

Indore is fast emerging as a rival to Kota, Rajasthan, as India's capital for coaching and exam preparation. As explained to me by the manager of a large coaching institute, the availability of 'big-city' amenities at 'small-city' prices is fuelling Indore's rise.

I was traveling all around Madhya Pradesh during the general elections, and I didn't have much time on my hands. So I hit the ground running. Soon after getting off my flight, I found myself at the local branch of a large chain of coaching centres. Most Indians have perhaps seen an advertisement for this chain, one of the country's largest coaching providers. Founded in the early 1990s, as India's economy liberalized, it has since expanded to almost 250 offices in 120 cities and towns, according to its website. I was there to ask the management if I could talk to some of the students to ask them about who they intended to vote for in the ongoing elections.

But I made a huge blunder. I told the branch manager, a man maybe ten or fifteen years older than me, that I was a journalist. In recent years, the coaching industry has come under the scanner. Journalists and authorities are increasing their scrutiny of these for-profit education providers, and I think the manager didn't want a reporter snooping around his jurisdiction. After interrogating me for fifteen minutes, he got quite worked up and asked me to leave, which I did.

However, neither the manager nor the company owned the parking lot outside the centre, where I started approaching students leaving the facility.

They were preparing for the CAT, or Common Admission Test examination. They were all keen to get admitted into an IIM, though none of them had thought about what career they might want to pursue after graduating. As I was beginning to talk to my third interviewee, a twenty-one-year-old woman from Chitrakoot, a small town in Madhya Pradesh, the branch manager reappeared. He had brought a security guard with him. He immediately intervened, ordering the student to stop talking to me. The manager was visibly agitated by my presence near his centre and told me he would get me thrown out of the parking lot, which is when his guard started moving closer toward me. He even hurled some mother-sister abuses my way to register his anger. Even though I was on public property and well within my legal rights to be there, I retreated.

I didn't want to create a ruckus and since I was outnumbered, I decided to move on. I knew I would need to change my strategy to approach the other coaching centres on my list.

Coaching in India has become a huge business. Technopak Advisors, a consulting firm, estimated the size of the industry to be approximately $7.5 billion in 2019, up from roughly $2 billion in 2008.[23] That puts it at an annual growth rate of roughly 16 per cent, perhaps making coaching one of the fastest growing industries in the country.

The coaching industry is wide-ranging and diverse. It equips students to take almost all college entrance tests from the JEE for engineering schools to the CLAT for law schools, the NEET for medical colleges and the SAT and TOEFL for those planning to go abroad. It also covers the entire gamut of management courses, such as the CAT and the GMAT, along with professional courses such as the infamous Chartered Accountancy (CA) test. The acronyms are endless. Coaching centres even train students to become Company Secretaries (CS) and Bank POs, that is, probationary officers. And then there's coaching to crack the most sought-after exam of them all: the UPSC, to become a gazetted government officer.

Adjusting my strategy, I decided to adopt a new name, Vivan Malhotra, and pretend I was looking at coaching for myself. My next stop was Resonance, a local branch of a coaching operation headquartered in Kota. Telling the receptionist I was interested in CA/CS courses, I was swiftly ushered into a CCTV-surveilled room with an admissions counsellor. In hindsight, I should have looked up what CS courses were before walking in. In the United States and pretty much everywhere else, CS is shorthand for computer science. In India's coaching lingo, it refers to Company Secretary. This dawned on me soon after she started talking, telling me how I could become a CS without a college degree. Luckily, she hadn't picked up on my duplicity and continued, telling me about the three tiers of CS positions, the salaries available afterwards, and what it would take for me to become a company secretary. Processing this information overload, I told the admissions counsellor I would be back soon and made a quick run for the exit.

I continue to get calls from Resonance, each offering me a new discount or class package.

The coaching industry exists because of a warped supply and demand problem in 21ˢᵗ Century India. The population has swelled, making the country one of the youngest in the world, but the supply of good quality schools, colleges and universities has stagnated if not declined. Given that economic opportunity is so closely linked to educational qualification, getting into a top college, and later, government service, becomes the ultimate goal not just for students, but even their extended families.

This is one of the reasons Indore is booming. Students often move to the city with either one or both parents, essentially creating a demand for a wide range of complementary services to serve the coaching industry: from hostels to meal providers.

Entrance tests exist all over the world and India is no exception. The acceptance rates for elite institutions can often be close to 2 per cent. For example, roughly 190,000 people took the CAT examination in 2020 for 4,500 seats in post-graduate diploma courses at the IIMs.[24] For 11,000 seats at the

IITs, almost 161,000 people appeared for the first two papers of the JEE Advanced in 2019.[25]

Traditional schools, public and private, are no longer seen as sufficient to train their students in getting into an IIT or a top medical college. Coaching centres are therefore filling this void, and in many parts of the country, have replaced schools. Students can now obtain their school degree from their coaching centre itself.

Some attribute this to a focus by state and central education boards on increasing their enrolment ratio at the expense of quality and learning outcomes. Students finish their school becoming experts at memorizing texts but fail to apply concepts they have learned towards problem solving, which is what the JEE, and the modern economy, requires.

Indore was the first city in India to house both an IIT and an IIM, developing a reputation as a growing academic centre. It now also hosts corporate campuses for two of India's IT giants: Infosys and Tata Consultancy Services.

However, Indore's prosperity has not translated into widespread employment. It has instead created an important challenge: a rising number of aspirational young adults and millennials who find themselves unqualified for the few jobs that are available. Madhya Pradesh's labour ministry data put the unemployment rate in the state at 43 per cent in 2015–16, and a 2017 state economic survey found that more than 1.4 million local youth (aged 20–29 years) were unemployed, of whom 1.29 million were educated.[26]

Looking for young voters in the run up to the elections, I spent an afternoon at Indore's famous Devi Ahilya Vishwavidyalaya (DAVV) campus, speaking to students about their political views and economic aspirations. The campus seemed largely deserted even though classes were in session, so I made my way to the canteen, hoping to find students to interview. The canteen was more of a tea stall with a shed over it, and I saw a few groups of students at tables; in most of the groups, the students were watching videos with each other on their smartphones. Confident I wasn't interrupting any serious discussions or academic projects, I approached one group of friends. It was equally divided in terms of gender, and everyone was from Madhya Pradesh. They told me they were all studying computer science to find a job in the private sector. It took me a few minutes to break the ice and convince these people that I was simply trying to know their aspirations and anxieties before they got candid with me.

As we started talking, one thing soon became clear: None of them was optimistic about their employment prospects. 'Neither TCS nor Infosys will hire us. They only hire south Indians because they are more qualified, and even if they did hire locally, there are too many students for them to absorb,' a young man in a group of engineering students told me.

'The IT sector doesn't exist in Madhya Pradesh at all,' he continued, pointing out the lack of opportunities for engineering and computer science graduates in the state.

These were middle class students from Indore and neighbouring districts, who had resigned themselves to moving out of the state once they were done studying.

Even though Infosys has a new campus in town, lured by generous incentives offered by the state government and the city's growing economic power, locals do not have a hometown advantage owing to its central hiring process. This means that they aren't competing against other engineers from Indore or Madhya Pradesh, but a national talent pool.

The distorted supply and demand problem in education and population created another problem: a boom in substandard private engineering colleges and MBA programmes. Small town India is full of these, and I saw some in Indore and Bhopal. These were engineering colleges which were maybe one or two rooms in a commercial complex. My driver in Bhopal, which was my next stop, had been to one of these. He had received his MBA from Dus Number (Number 10) market in Bhopal, where his college was located. It had since shut down, replaced by a pharmacy.

How does this affect millennials? You might ask. This was one of the reasons I sought a meeting with Pratap Nair, the founder of First Jobzz, a placement agency in Indore which runs a bevy of training programmes to train people in acquiring technical and soft skills they may not have picked up at college. In forty hours of classroom instruction, its 'Fluence' module, intended for people of any age, helps students with their communication skills (teaching them basic grammar, sentence construction and vocabulary), develop their personality and etiquette, work on their body language, and improve their public speaking ability. It also operates other coaching programmes for current college students to help them find jobs, and for school students hoping to become lawyers.

After climbing three floors of a commercial building to get to the corporate office of First Jobzz, which has three centres scattered around Indore, I waited for Nair. He was busy helping students prepare for an upcoming examination and I was grateful for the hour he was able to spare for me.

A Kerala native who made Madhya Pradesh his home, Nair rejected the notion that there was an unemployment crisis in the country, arguing instead that it was an employability crisis. 'There is a gap between what companies want and the skills which colleges are teaching,' he said and went on to describe how schools and colleges in Madhya Pradesh and all over India, were not teaching their students skills that would make them employable.

'Jobs exist but there are huge gaps in skilling. Roughly 800–1000 people come to me every year and about 60 per cent get jobs after training at First Jobzz,' he said. Many of his students go on to work in banks or take up administrative positions at private companies. Technically, they could get these jobs even after their basic matriculation, but First Jobzz essentially provides school-level education, often even after students graduate college, to make up for the gaps in skilling and learning.

Public engineering colleges in Madhya Pradesh are using curricula developed more than fifteen years ago, when flip phones were in vogue and 2G technology was the next-big-thing. Although private colleges have a better track record in updating syllabi, the low standard of entry requirements makes it hard to attract and develop top quality talent. Students from these institutions therefore don't have the skills they need to get hired by IT or engineering companies, making them turn to agencies like First Jobzz to become employable.

The education industry is one of the reasons Indore is one of the youngest cities in Madhya Pradesh. Its fast-multiplying exam institutes and placement agencies are attracting droves of youth in hopes of getting an education or becoming employable, responsibilities which the state has inadvertently ceded to the private sector. It is not a city where you will find hordes of young Indians shuttling to office buildings in professional clothing, but students enrolled at coaching centres or engineering colleges spending their free time at kulfi stalls and pakora sellers.

This is a national problem. Either due to excessive regulation or the lack of appetite, or often both, colleges have effectively given up on improving the quality of education they provide.

New technologies and techniques are slow to be introduced, and innovation is kept at a far distance. Due to the excessive privatization of higher education and the incentive for profit making, teachers are not compensated well, therefore the best talent is usually never in front of the classroom. In fact, one engineering teacher I met on one of my trips had previously failed his final examination as a student. He took another year, barely scraped by, and immediately began teaching students engineering. He had no idea what AI or machine learning were. I don't think I need to say more about the quality of instruction he was providing.

~

'Islands of California in a Sea of Sub-Saharan Africa'

These are the words used by Amartya Sen and his frequent collaborator Jean Drèze to describe India in their book *An Uncertain Glory: India and its Contradictions*, a study of the extreme wealth and extreme poverty that co-exist in the country today.[27]

Their statement played back in my head, almost like *déjà vu*, as I visited the Infosys headquarters in Bangalore and their campus in Mysore. With seed capital of just $250, seven engineers huddled together in 1981 in Pune to form a company known as Infosys Consultants. They didn't even own a single computer for their first two years of operations, because they didn't have enough clients and the arduous regulations on importing foreign computers in socialist India further compounded matters. In 1983, they signed their first client, Data Basics Corporation in New York, developing software solutions for its business processes.

From there, they never looked back. New clients signed on, and once India's economy was liberalized in 1991, the company's global ambitions were unrestricted. In 2004, Infosys crossed $1 billion in revenue, with over two-thirds coming from the United States, where it serviced clients such as Boeing, Reebok and Visa.[28]

Today, Infosys has more than 200,000 employees scattered across hundreds of offices in more than thirty countries spread over four continents.

It was a rainy morning in August 2018 when I first set foot inside the Infosys headquarters in Bangalore's Electronic City. I was staying with a friend near the airport, and anyone familiar with the geography of Bangalore and its horrendous traffic would know that I had a two-and-a-half-hour journey from the airport to Electronic City. The intermittent rains created numerous potholes which only worsened the city's notorious traffic problems, and a long-delayed under-construction metro system added to the prevailing sense of chaos.

But the moment I walked through the heavily secured gates of the Infosys headquarters, it was as if I had entered a different country, or even civilization, altogether. Within minutes, the chaos and hustle of Bangalore's roads were a distant memory. I was there to meet Mr Binod Hampapur, Executive Vice President and Global Head of Talent and Technology Operations at Infosys, who had arranged for me to first take a tour of the headquarters and then spend three days at the Infosys campus in Mysore.

Given the size of the headquarters, spread across more than 80 acres, my hosts had graciously provided me with a golf cart and personal guide to show me around. As we began the tour, I was told that no outside vehicles, with the exception of ambulances and security vehicles, were allowed inside the campus. That's probably why I saw so many people on foot or on bicycle. One of the first things shown on the tour were the first buildings that were constructed in the 1980s. Simply designed, and built using red brick, they've become somewhat of a historical monument at the Infosys headquarters, a reminder of the humble origins of the company.

The campus itself was incredible, similar to what I had seen at the Google headquarters in Mountain View, California. I saw multiple food courts, a giant laundry facility, gymnasiums, tennis, badminton, and volleyball courts, a swimming pool, the famous pyramid-shaped media centre where Infosys releases its annual results, and a set of buildings with a giant circular shaped hole in the middle—to resemble a human eye—from which the campus looked out onto Bangalore. I heard all about the amenities and recreational facilities on offer. As my tour guide told me, Infosys founder Narayana Murthy once called the assets of his company not its buildings, technologies, or patents, but its people. And as its people left work every day in the evening, the company had to figure out how to bring them back, so it built an elaborate and extraordinary campus of facilities to enhance productivity and keep its employees happy.

While getting lunch at one of the employee food courts, a group of engineers sitting next to me were discussing how to code a program for one of their clients, and finding common ground on which method to choose. At another table, I saw a group of foreign interns, part of the Infosys InStep program which brings students primarily from the US and England to work on Infosys projects in India. I was told that on any given day of the week, food courts on the campus would have a cuisine of the week—Gujarati, South Indian, Punjabi, Chinese, among others—giving employees a truly huge slate of options to eat from.

After lunch, I called an Uber to make my 3 p.m. train to Mysore, where I would spend the next three days at the Infosys campus, which is essentially a second stage of university for its new hires. After graduating from college, new recruits at Infosys spend anywhere between nineteen and twenty-five weeks in Mysore, where they take part in a foundation programme to get trained and skilled to join the company. Different from a traditional university, they get paid to attend these lessons as regular employees but must successfully complete the curriculum in twenty-five weeks, or be released from their employment contract.

My Uber driver didn't need Google Maps to find his way to the giant Infosys campus in Mysore. About twenty minutes from the station, most taxi and auto drivers in town know exactly how to get there. Sprawled across more than 330 acres, the campus is like a self-contained city. Given that it essentially serves as a university for new hires, it houses ninety-five residential buildings, 10,095 rooms, and 16,485 beds, in addition to numerous software development blocks, learning centres and recreational facilities.

The campus was like a cocoon, totally separated from the world outside its walls, truly like an island of California. While Mysore itself is a well-governed and clean city, the moment I walked through the big gates, I once again felt that I was in a totally foreign country. As I was taken to my room in a golf cart, I really didn't know where to look: at the futuristic orb-shaped multiplex complex; a software development block designed to resemble an origami design; some incredible flora; or whether to just observe the throngs of new hires who were leaving their classrooms after 5.30 p.m., chatting and cracking jokes as they walked purposefully to their next destination.

Once I settled into my assigned room, I went through the information packet on my desk. There was a list of facilities and a bunch of statistics about the campus—which I was going to see during a campus tour the next day—but I soon realized, as mentioned in the packet, that it truly was 'the ultimate university campus'. You didn't need to leave for anything. It had everything any young Indian could want.

As I got in the golf cart for a campus tour the next day, I didn't expect it to last longer than forty-five minutes. I was in for a pleasant surprise. My guide began by showing me one of the ten artificial lakes at Infosys Mysore, which the company had dug to irrigate its lands and recharge the groundwater. All of the lakes were protected areas, so no one was allowed in, but for the ducks and other birds that were frolicking in the water as we drove by. We stopped at a building overlooking a lake with a gym on the first floor, and a golf simulator on the ground level. It was built after clients complained that the campus had everything but a golf course. I was allowed to see the bedrooms allotted to new hires, each of which had two comfortable beds, desks, a television and a well-equipped bathroom. After observing the famous orb-shaped Infosys multiplex from the outside, I went inside to see the largest of its four auditoriums, which can seat 1024 people. I was told that new hires could watch most new releases at the multiplex for a subscription of just Rs 100 for the entire month, a fraction of the cost of a ticket for one movie at a multiplex in any major Indian city. I was then shown the recreation centre, which housed an eight-lane bowling alley, swimming pool, squash, tennis and badminton courts better than any I had seen before. There was a yoga studio, a music room, a massive gym, a bank and a convenience store. All of these facilities are available for new hires to use once they finished their daily classes at 5.30 p.m.

What was perhaps the crown-jewel of my two-hour long campus tour was the Global Education Center 2, inaugurated in 2009 by Sonia Gandhi. Designed using the US Capitol, St. Paul's Cathedral in London and the Rashtrapati Bhavan in India as inspiration, the building is enormous. With a built-up area of over a million square feet, it can accommodate 9,500 trainees in ninety-five training rooms and five examination rooms. It houses a giant library with over 80,000 books and has a capacity for an additional 20,000 books. I was truly in awe of this building. Nothing like it exists anywhere else in India. Not at the IITs or IIMs I visited, and definitely not at the next level of public or even private universities. This is at a completely different scale. The architecture, while not to my personal taste, is sweeping and commanding. Everything is fitted with state-of-the-art technologies. This is a place designed to boost morale and enhance learning.

I had gone to Infosys to learn more about its recruitment strategies, new hire training processes, and to talk to its millennial employees. What I found most interesting about Hampapur's comments to me the previous day in Bangalore was that when the company recruited fresh graduates, it did not look for a stellar academic record, but for academic consistency and learnability. 'Indian engineering institutes just deliver engineers into the system,' he told me. 'The engineers who graduate and come out know certain things which are far from what the industry needs. Infosys can either crib about this or do something about it,' he added.

So Infosys decided to do something about it. In addition to collaborating with certain universities and colleges to help them design engineering curricula, Infosys knew it needed to do more. In 2002, it established its foundation programme in Mysore, which began with fifty trainees, one trainer, and a single classroom.[29] Since then, it has trained 100,000 Infoscions and grown to become a giant university to educate and skill 15,000 new employees at any given time, making it the world's largest corporate training facility. None of this is cheap. An HR executive did a back-of-the-envelope estimate and told me that the company spends around Rs 5 lakh (approximately $9,000) on training each new hire. That's more than the cost of an entire education at most Indian universities. While Infosys views such expenditures as a small cost to maintain its supply of talent, I could not help but think that many first-time entrepreneurs and start-up would not be able afford to spend that kind of money on training new talent or spend more to hire better quality talent. The disadvantage could well put them out of business or stop their idea from ever taking off.

As I spoke to a panel of young new hires and lateral entries in training at Mysore, my view of the impact of India's education system on Indian millennials continued to get reinforced. One of my first questions, on whether they were satisfied with their college education, drew the same responses I was seeing all across the country. 'Not really. It was dull and boring,' a graduate from an engineering school in Kota, Rajasthan, told me. Another new recruit from Jabalpur, Madhya Pradesh, described how he felt that he was actually being tested for the first time in his life at Infosys—after graduating from college—because teachers at his institution used to give away the practical questions a day before the exam, effectively negating the need to study and prepare seriously for their examinations.

What began to stand out in these conversations was that Infosys was often not just 'training' them to do well at the company. It was, in fact, substituting for the traditional university. It was imparting skills that the new employees should have ordinarily learned at university. Since the universities it hires from—mid-tier technical institutes and colleges—were failing in providing a comprehensive education, Infosys had to step in and fix the problem for itself.

Walking around the Mysore campus often made me forget about the India outside the walls of the compound. All I could see were swarms of new employees, walking towards or back from their classrooms, in small groups, chatting and laughing with each other. I haven't seen anything else like this in India.

But it also signified something much more cynical and dark: the breakdown of higher education in India. The 200,000 people inside the Infosys campuses across India are a tiny fraction of the country's 1.3 billion (and rapidly expanding) population.

In the stories of Ravindra and Infosys, a common thread emerges: India's educational institutions are not teaching their students how to succeed.

Infosys provides its new hires with a cape of inclusion. It teaches them the skills they need to succeed at the workplace—capacities that should have been acquired at the university level. Infosys building its own university to train new hires is not an achievement of the country's success, but a symbol of its failure.

~

Over the decades, as the central government prioritized building IIMs and IITs while leaving primary education to state governments, what was produced was not just a deeply unequal system of education but, in many places, a foundation of low-quality education and vast regional inequalities. South and northeast India, where regional parties and local governments have had a better track record on human development indicators, have better education systems whose graduates find it easier to get well-paying jobs. It is not a surprise that most coders or engineers abroad are from Andhra Pradesh, a state that prioritized technical education fairly early; or that most nurses and doctors who migrate abroad are from Kerala, since the state has the best healthcare and education system in the country.

Indian families have long viewed education as a passport out of penury, yet political apathy and poor management by the state has kept much of Indian education at a substandard quality. As a result, the private sector has stepped in at every level of education and learning to fill in glaring gaps left by the state. From tutors for mathematics to coaching centres to prepare students for the IITs or IIMs to Infosys' six-month long bootcamp, the private sector has had to fill a crucial void left by the state. But it has only done so for families who have resources to pay for these tutors and coaches, in effect exacerbating an education system which filters students more than it teaches them.

And because the overall stock of talent in the country remains low, Indian millennials find themselves ill-equipped to innovate, start their own businesses or break into better lives.

ECONOMIC ASPIRATIONS

On 4 January 2019, *The Washington Post* reported a story that has become too familiar to most Indians. When 63,000 jobs opened in the country's railways, 19 million people applied.[1] The *Post* story followed another galling report by *The Economic Times* on how 93,000 people, including 3,700 PhD holders, 28,000 post-graduates, and 50,000 graduates applied for sixty-two government messenger positions in Uttar Pradesh.[2] The messenger position required a minimum education of class five and the hard-to-find skill of riding a bicycle.

Similarly, when the Mumbai police began a recruitment drive in 2018 to hire approximately 1100 constables, the junior-most officers in the police force, more than 200,000 people applied.[3] These included three doctors, five lawyers, 167 MBAs and 423 engineers. The minimum qualification required was completing higher secondary schooling, or the twelfth standard. Arup Patnaik, who had served as the city's Commissioner of Police in 2012 told the *Mumbai Mirror* newspaper that had reported the story: 'During my time as the CP, there were no applications from engineers or lawyers or doctors.' He added: 'There were a few postgraduates. The youth in Maharashtra are keen on government jobs. With the Make in India push, it is a sad reflection of our times that engineers are applying for this post, especially when there are so many infrastructural projects like the Metro and Coastal road.'[4]

However, the big story here isn't just the over qualification of people applying for these jobs, but the sheer number of people applying.

India has a long-standing love affair with government jobs. Their immense appeal traces back to the country's socialist past where the government controlled large chunks of the economy, and government and public sector employees effectively had job security until retirement. These positions had been seen as cushy gigs which were stable and generated a decent pension after retirement. It was as good as you could get in socialist India.

But what is behind the obsession with government jobs in 21st Century capitalist India?

The CSDS study found that 65 per cent of young Indians list a government job as their top choice for a career.[5] A far-behind second option, setting up one's own business, was the number one priority for just 19 per cent of the survey's respondents, followed by a job in the private sector, which only 7 per cent listed as their top choice. The survey also revealed that more than seven in ten respondents were anxious—approximately five in ten were highly so—about jobs and employment.[6] Almost a third listed their occupation as 'student', twice the percentage that did so when the survey was previously conducted in 2007.[7]

When I first read these survey findings before I began my field research, I had a hard time believing them. How could fewer than one in ten Indians say that a private sector job was their top priority while almost seven in ten wanted a government job? Surely those numbers were in reverse.

But it took me just one trip out of Delhi to encounter the sobering reality of India's obsession with government jobs.

•————————•

Sarkar Raj

Gagan is a 24-year-old courier and supervisor at a logistics company in Bhopal, Madhya Pradesh. Originally from Guna district in the state, Gagan comes from a family of barbers. His father, grandfather and other forefathers had all been barbers. This isn't a surprise to anyone familiar with the Indian caste system in which an individual's profession is preordained before they are born. Since he was from a family of barbers, he belonged to the Nai caste, which was classified as an 'Other Backward Class' (OBC) in Madhya Pradesh.

After finishing his schooling, he got into Rajiv Gandhi Technological University in Bhopal through a quota for OBCs. After his father's death at the end of his first year, Gagan, being the eldest son, needed to find a job to help his family. His teachers worked out a way for him to stay enrolled and maintain a full-time job. They told him he did not need to attend any classes, and only had to show up for his exams. He would pass despite his actual performance. Gagan got lucky in that he did not need to sacrifice his education to support his family.

Gagan managed to graduate with a B.Tech in engineering—making him the first in his family to finish school or college—but without the education or skills of an actual engineer. He was, therefore, an engineer only on paper. His job as a courier at the logistics company paid him about Rs 10,000 a month, a wage that had become difficult to support his growing family.

Extremely street savvy, Gagan rose through the ranks of his company, becoming a supervisor in less than two years.

But with a wife and daughter to feed, and another child on the way, Gagan's salary would not be sufficient for much longer. When I met him, he was desperate to find something more lucrative.

Gagan is not alone. What is often forgotten when we consider the economic aspirations of Indian millennials is that when compared to young people globally, the average Indian millennial has more responsibilities and dependents to think about. According to 2011 Census data, the median age at marriage was 22.8 years for men and 19.2 years for women.[8] The median age at marriage for graduates and above was 24.6 years, five years more than the number for illiterates. And among urban men and women, the median was 24.5 years and 19.9 years respectively.[9]

These numbers are important. They tell us that young Indians today don't have just themselves to think about—they often have a spouse and children to consider when making important economic decisions. When I first met him, Gagan had begun preparing to take the Madhya Pradesh Public Service Commission (MPPSC) examination. He was enrolled at a coaching centre in the Dus Number market in Bhopal, where an instructor had rented out a single office room to give lessons to Gagan and others like him who wanted a government job. He paid this instructor Rs 1500 a month, 15 per cent of his salary. Though Gagan recognized he could possibly rise up in the private sector, he felt that he would not be able to ascend beyond a certain point and was worried about being laid off at any time or losing his livelihood if the economy went south. He wanted more stability in his finances, and a government job was the only option for him to get a sense of economic security. Gagan also knew he couldn't send his children to a good school or give them a better life than his, on the salary of a courier. He also had hopes of reforming the system; he told me of his grand plans of eradicating laziness and corruption from the bureaucracy if he cleared the examination. Since he got his degree, he had not once considered getting a job even vaguely related to his education as an engineer.

'Why would I want to stay in the private sector?' he asked me as a matter of fact. 'I could get fired at any time. I found this job with great difficulty and finding a new job when I am older will be even harder for me. A government job is a job for life, and it will give me and my family dignity we never had. After retirement, I will get a pension too.'

He continued to ask me, 'How will I feed my children or marry my daughter off? I will never be able to make ends meet as a courier.'

Gagan is not alone. Millions of young Indians believe that a private sector job could evaporate with a change in political weather or economic climate. Instead, they would rather take a safer government job.

~

One-Way Ticket

In small towns and villages, the District Collector acquires an emperor-like status and personality.

They are the ultimate decision makers for regular people. They travel around with an air of authority and have the power to take decisions of great importance for the localities they serve. The fact that they are fairly young, around thirty-five, when they reach the District Collector position, only emphasizes the prestige and upward mobility imbued in the Indian Administrative Service. Every young person who has regular interactions with the district level of government, like millions of Indians in rural and small-town India, has seen a demonstration of the District Collector's power. Joining the civil services, in any capacity, is therefore viewed as the ultimate achievement for a young person, and youth are conditioned to view these positions as the only kinds of employment opportunities worth seeking.

But statistically, with an acceptance rate which hovers around 0.002 per cent, the likelihood that an average young Indian will join the IAS is incredibly low. Nevertheless, in the last three decades, a sprawling industry of the Union Public Service Commission (UPSC) examination preparation academies and coaching centres have taken off. These individuals spend some of the best years of their lives preparing for this test, most of them doing no other work than studying for multiple hours every day.

Talking to former bureaucrats and diplomats who joined the government services between the 1950s and the 1990s, one thing became clear: Most hadn't attended IAS academies or taken classes. They studied on their own, using a few specialized textbooks, and did not need dedicated coaches or training centres to help them pass the UPSC examination. The breakdown of public education mentioned in the previous chapter and the lack of lucrative jobs in the private sector, along with a massive boom in the country's population, has resulted in millions of Indians spending their time studying for one or another exam and created an entire industry dedicated to coaching and exam training. There are too many people competing for too few good jobs.

In October 2018, I met Vinita, a twenty-five-year-old resident of Delhi's Safdarjung Enclave. Her father was a household cook originally from Uttarakhand, and she lived with her family in the staff quarters provided by his employer. She had been preparing for the UPSC examination for four years, having taken and failed the test twice already. The social protection offered by a government job is particularly attractive to young women like her, who do not find it easy to gain employment in manufacturing or service sector jobs.

She wanted to give it one last shot before her parents started looking for a boy for her to marry. Vinita had been sponsored by her father's employer to attend a private school in Delhi, and she did well enough in her board examinations to study history at Ram Lal Anand College at Delhi University's South Campus. She had around three to four hours of class every day, but she only needed to be physically present for attendance. Being in the classroom didn't mean much; teachers would essentially go over the assigned textbooks word-for-word, so she didn't miss anything by skipping class. Vinita had a carefully planned routine—she would essentially just make an appearance at college to mark her attendance, and then leave. On some days, she would have to make two trips to college, but she found the hassle worth the extra time to use towards studying for the UPSC. As a result, her schedule gave her plenty of time to take IAS coaching classes on the side.

Her entire life, Vinita's parents had struggled so she could achieve her dreams and propel her family firmly into India's middle class. She was told that there was nothing she could not achieve if she worked hard. 'My parents worked so that I could study and become an IAS officer,' she told me, talking about her years-long preparation to clear one of India's most gruelling examinations. Vinita would spend ten to thirteen hours a day studying. It had become her life's sole purpose. In five years, she saw one movie—*Dangal*, on her birthday in December 2016—

when her friends forced her to spend some time away from her books.

The first time she took the exam, her score was not high enough. She believed she didn't make it because she had not gone to the right coaching centre. So, for her second attempt in 2017, she moved to Chanakya IAS academy. Its fees—more than Rs 1 lakh—amounted to what her father made in about eight months of work. He took a loan from his employer to help pay for Vinita's coaching classes. It was a huge financial investment, but the thinking at home was that the return would be worth it. But once again, she did not make it through.

'My family is drowning in debt', she said. 'I am going to study on my own one last time. I have to make it through now. I don't know what I will do if I don't clear the test. I will have to get married.'

In 2017, 450,000 Indians sat for the UPSC exam, hoping to make it to the next round and to eventually secure a place in one of the twenty-six government services the examination screens for.[10] Only 990 made it, a success rate of 0.002 per cent. Vinita was not one of them. She had hoped that her third time would be a charm and tried not to think of a future where she had not cleared the exam. Her mother told me they would try to get her married as soon as possible if it didn't work out.

For Vinita, the idea of a government job had meant everything. There was the lure of stability until she retired, allowing her to support her parents. It would also give her and her family immense prestige, making them the first in their village and community to send a child into the gazetted government services. On an individual level, becoming a government servant would give Vinita autonomy and personal freedom that her alternative option, arranged marriage, would not. Although she would have to get married eventually, she believed she would get better matches and wield greater power in her marriage if she were a government officer. A public sector job is incredibly valuable in India's marriage market, where families prioritize economic stability almost as much as caste compatibility.

She didn't see a government job as just a job. She saw it as *a one-way ticket to a better life* and possibly her only opportunity to get there.

Government jobs have *always* been sought after in India. For more than four decades after Independence, the country's economy was closed off to the outside world and the private sector offered few alternatives, but if you had a PhD or an MBA, applying for the position of a peon would have been unfathomable. This is also due to the historical, and in many ways, continuing stranglehold of the caste system in the country, where dominant castes enjoyed greater access to good quality education and employment. With the implementation of the Mandal Commission report in 1990, and liberalization in 1991, many dominant castes, particularly those in urban areas or with good education, began to exit the public sector space, trading government positions for economic power. To the hundreds of millions of OBCs, an easier pathway to gazetted government jobs gave them opportunities to access power and dignity for the first time in independent India.[11]

Vinita is one of these young Indians. Her father's parents were too poor to give him an education, but he was able to provide his daughter with one. She now wants to take that forward and build a life for her family—which, as far as she could see, would only be possible if she secured a government job.

And this is one of the reasons she invested so much in this one potential opportunity: India has simply failed to create enough positions to employ the millions joining its workforce every month. There aren't enough jobs to absorb the approximately 1.3 million Indians who become of working age every month and help them make a living, much less give them upward mobility.[12] This problem, known as India's 'jobless growth', has been discussed in numerous articles, studies, and books, and it has tremendous direct and indirect repercussions.[13] The unmet aspirations and social anxiety of being unemployed deprive Indian millennials crucial social and economic agency their counterparts in other parts of the world enjoy and often take for granted.

And most jobs being created in India are on the lower end of the skills and earnings' totem pole. In its household survey, the Centre for Monitoring Indian Economy found that as young people attained more education, the number of jobs commensurate to their skills and knowledge only reduced. In the three-year period from early 2016 to late 2018, it found that jobs for those who had only completed their primary education— until the fifth grade—had grown by 45 per cent. In contrast, jobs for those who had a secondary education—until the tenth, eleventh or twelfth grade—only grew by 12 per cent.[14]

Additionally, while the CMIE survey found that employment in India had shrunk by roughly ten million jobs between 2016 and 2018, the number of self-employed individuals had actually increased by 20 million.[15] But these self-employed people actually came from some of the most vulnerable economic groups such as street vendors selling cigarettes or frying pakoras, and hand-cart operators. Although CMIE data cannot and should not be taken as gospel, and the individuals surveyed were not only millennials, the study clearly found that India's GDP growth has failed to result in the widespread growth of well-paying sustainable jobs. This is a problem which most acutely affects millennials, who are trying to move up and consolidate their position in the economy.

The CSDS study found that since 2007, when the survey was last conducted, preference for a government job among graduates had *increased* by almost 20 percentage points, while the preference for private jobs had *declined* by 16.[16] In 2007, almost half of those surveyed listed a government job as their preference, while a quarter listed private employment. In 2016, 73 per cent, or three quarters had given *sarkari naukris* as their top preference, while those who preferred private employment had fallen to single digit, at 9 per cent.

In terms of the current occupational profile of India's youth, the survey found that the most common activity occupying India's youth was education, with a third (32 per cent) of those surveyed describing their occupation as 'student'. This figure had more than doubled since 2007, and it stood at just 13 per cent. Indore's education economy is a by-product of this boom in higher education and coaching, and Vinita is among the millions in this growing segment.

But young Indians are engaged in what seems to be a never-ending cycle of education, not because they want to learn more but because they are desperate to increase their employability. Anything that might help them find a job is a solution that must be considered. And they find themselves in this situation because of the shortcomings of the Indian education system. The graduates from these institutions are simply not qualified for most jobs in the 21st Century knowledge economy.

~

During India's socialist period, the private sector was never allowed or enabled to become the predominant engine of economic growth. State control over the economy was vast and government-run enterprises operated in nearly every sector. Furthermore, India prioritized capital-heavy industrialization instead of labour-intensive manufacturing, encumbering the creation of a vibrant base of blue-collar factory jobs which allowed other nations to expand their middle class and move towards higher levels of income.

India's economic reforms took place in 1991, three decades ago. They unshackled the country's formal sector, creating new sunrise industries in information technology and services, and ushered in unprecedented levels of foreign investment. Colaba and Connaught Place were replaced by Bandra Kurla Complex, Gurgaon, Hi-Tech City, and Whitefield as the new hotbeds of financial power. The job market became more diverse, giving educated young Indians options beyond medicine or government services as viable career paths. New television channels opened for the first time, and foreign money flowed into the country, helping finance new suburbs, cities, corporations and lifestyles.

However, instead of shifting the bulk of India's workforce from the farm to the factory, liberalization did not go beyond enabling the expansion of formal and service sectors. It is remarkable that the manufacturing sector's contribution to the country's GDP has remained unchanged since the introduction of reforms.[17] Without a doubt, liberalization created enclaves of incredible wealth and opportunity in largely urbanized areas, while the rest of the country was expected to grow from the trickled down wealth. And although substantial wealth did trickle down, helping to lift millions out of poverty, the job market—still dominated by informal work—did not evolve to keep pace with India's population boom.

With the failure of these, and subsequent economic reforms, to create a new quantum of manufacturing jobs in the country, government jobs continue to remain the most sought-after form of employment. This is and will remain a huge challenge for the country, not only because government jobs are limited and should remain limited, but because at a deeper level, the economy has structurally failed to generate vibrant employment opportunities for the country's youth, thereby crippling its 'demographic dividend'. In December 2018, former RBI governor and IMF Chief Economist Raghuram Rajan cited an incident in which 25 million people applied for 90,000 railway jobs as evidence for the fact that India was simply not creating enough jobs for its young.[18] A month later, in January 2019, the *Business Standard* newspaper broke an explosive story. It published a leaked report by the National Sample Survey Office, a government body, which found that unemployment in India had reached a 45-year high.

The report also contained an alarming finding: Youth unemployment was 'much higher compared to that in the overall population'.[19] It also found that the labour force participation rate, or the share of the population either employed or available for employment, had fallen to 49.8 per cent in 2017–18, down from 55.9 per cent in 2011–12. This means that an entire *half* of India's working age population (15 years and above) was not contributing to any economic activity.[20]

The NSSO and its annual survey, considered the gold standard of employment data in India, soon came under attack from the ruling BJP. That he would create millions of jobs was one of the signature promises of Narendra Modi in his 2014 election, and any data that showed he wasn't succeeding became a political problem which needed to be neutralized. Two non-government members of the National Statistical Commission resigned from their positions, claiming the government had sidelined them and was trying to suppress the release of the data.[21] The Vice Chairman of the government's think tank, NITI Aayog, Dr Rajiv Kumar called a press conference, seeking to discredit the study by casting doubt on its methodology.[22]

On 31 May 2019, merely days after Prime Minister Modi's reelection, the labour ministry quietly released its employment data. Its figures matched those of the leaked NSSO report which the *Business Standard* published and also showed that unemployment was at a 45-year high.[23] The irony was lost on no one.

~

'You Might Be Suffering from Capitalism'

To get a better understanding of some of the academic research on India's unemployment, I found myself in Delhi's Jawaharlal Nehru University. Attacked by members of the right for its history of leftist activism and student agitations against the policies of the Modi government, I found the campus somewhat lived up to its reputation as a breeding ground of socialist and leftist thought. Posters asked students whether they felt 'sad and depressed', telling them they 'might be suffering from capitalism'. Symptoms of their illness might include: 'homelessness, unemployment, poverty, hunger, feelings of powerlessness/worthlessness, alienation, fear, apathy, boredom, cultural decay, loss of identity, doing things mostly for the sake of your CV, neglecting your health, feeling guilty for reading, extreme self-consciousness, loss of free speech, incarceration, suicidal or revolutionary thoughts'.

I was there to meet Dr Himanshu, a Professor of Economics and prominent newspaper columnist. He offered one possible explanation for India's continued obsession with government jobs: the exploitative nature of lower-level jobs in the private sector. As shopping malls and supermarkets continue to mushroom in Indian cities, they do indeed increase employment. But the employment they offer, such as low-level opportunities for sales attendants or store clerks, are inherently exploitative. Employees usually work twelve-hour shifts for low salaries and no additional benefits such as insurance or paid time off. Many retail outlets do not even have chairs for workers to rest. Since India's manufacturing sector is tiny compared to its service sector, jobs in the latter are far more ubiquitous, but far less desirable.

Prof. Himanshu went further, backdropping India's employment situation against the global economic climate, where cost-cutting has become the norm for companies and countries to remain competitive. Since fixed costs and raw materials prices cannot be reduced, the only way to trim expenses is to cut wage costs and employee benefits. Therefore, for a company to withstand competition, it is forced to keep its labour costs as low as possible, either by hiring fewer workers, paying workers less, or by working the same employees for longer periods of time.

Work conditions in the gig economy, which sprang out of developments in technology in the 21st Century, further exemplify the exploitative nature of job growth in India. The gig economy became ubiquitous with the rise of Uber as a ride-sharing service in the United States, where people with extra time on their hands could drive their personal vehicles for the company, transporting users booked through a mobile application. In India, driving for Uber or its local rival, Ola, is a full-time profession, where the companies even offer financing options for drivers to buy taxis for them to drive. Similarly, the growth of Zomato and Swiggy have created an explosion in jobs for delivery executives, who were previously hired directly, in smaller numbers, by restaurants and fast-food chains.

But the gig economy is not large or vibrant enough to absorb every millennial joining the workforce or looking for stable employment. The gig economy took off because it worked for a certain segment of the American population that either had one job that didn't pay enough or that was looking for temporary work. These jobs were never structured to become lifetime employment.

Despite that, these gig economy jobs have become full-time careers for millions in India. Even though I have yet to encounter an Indian millennial who aspires to drive for Uber or deliver food for Zomato, millions do so as full-time occupations, and will continue to do so as long as the platforms they serve remain economically viable.

Instead, I have met countless gig economy workers, including Uber drivers, Zomato delivery 'executives', and other such contractual workers who work twelve to fifteen hours every day, but are barely able to make ends meet. Consider the case of Sajid, an Uber driver I interviewed in Delhi. He told me he needed to work twelve to thirteen hours every day to earn about Rs 40,000 a month. Besides, he doesn't get to keep all his income. More than half goes in just running his car: paying off its loan, buying gas, insurance, maintenance expenses. He then has to spend money on rent, other household expenses and medical bills. At the end of the month, he's lucky if is left with Rs 1000.

And Sajid was among the better-off Uber drivers I interviewed while writing this book.

After dropping out of school, Sajid began working at the age of fifteen. He worked at a sari factory in Meerut for five years, before he was laid off as part of the company's cost-cutting measures. His father and brothers are all farmers. Since he lived at home, he was usually left with some extra money to spend, despite a low salary. But after being laid off, due to the lack of alternative employment at home, he took a loan and started driving for Uber in Delhi. When he first joined the platform, generous incentives and fewer drivers meant he made much more money than he does now — almost Rs 50,000 a month — for less work. He worked six days a week, for about ten hours every day. He hadn't considered any skilling or vocational programmes, since relatives who had attended those were still out of jobs. And in his early years as an Uber driver, he earned more than enough.

'Life was great when I first joined Uber in 2014. I made almost double what I make today. I had extra money to give to my wife and send to my family,' Sajid told me.

Soon the incentives began to disappear, and the costs started to increase. The job stopped bringing in the kind of money it did earlier. The laws of supply and demand soon caught up, and as thousands more across the country began to buy cars and start driving for Uber or Ola, the companies didn't need to lure drivers with generous incentives any longer. Drivers had to work longer hours for less money. Sajid also complained about not getting any time for himself and his wife. His health problems had increased due to body aches from driving, and he was constantly exhausted.

A well-placed Uber executive, on the condition of anonymity, explained to me in an interview that there were two broad categories of Uber drivers: those who drive for survival, and those who drive for surplus. The former are largely migrants to bigger cities who don't often own the cars they drive and spend longer hours on the road. These are the people who live hand to mouth and any external factor—be it driver strikes or gas price increases—impacts them significantly. Many of them drive for larger fleet operators and earn a flat figure for every trip they make, so they prefer doing shorter trips to make money faster.

But these aren't the only numbers Uber keeps track of. In fact, the company carefully tracks its drivers' earnings, particularly watching out if the monthly income of its median driver drops below what is internally called BRL, or below red line. Depending on the city and the amount of time drivers spend on the platform, a certain figure is considered the minimum income that is sustainable for a driver, and thus likely to keep them working for Uber. Anything below is considered BRL, and if the driver's income drops below that line, the company stops onboarding new drivers, essentially regulating supply and demand.

That minimum figure can be as low as Rs 14,000 a month in Kolkata and touch Rs 20,000 in Delhi. These are significant sums of money in the context of the broader economy, which is simply not creating enough jobs, let alone high-wage jobs. For the millions who are leaving behind the unpredictable nature of agriculture in India, driving for Uber is an opportunity to join city life and earn a decent wage, regardless of the low standard of living that the wage offers.

However, as the executive acknowledged, Uber's practices become problematic when seen from the promise of the gig economy.

People like Sajid and Ravindra are never going to make money off Uber. Large teams of engineers sitting in Gurugram, Bengaluru, Hyderabad and Silicon Valley, who keep meticulous track of statistics to ensure that drivers do not get rich, and that the one entity that profits from their labour is Uber. But this problem isn't just Uber's creation; it is part and parcel of the gig economy. When Zomato rolled out its new policy in 2019 to provide $1000 for every new child an employee had, as well as 26 weeks of paid parental leave, including to new fathers, it didn't mean *all* employees. It was only meant for its 5000-odd corporate employees, and not the 180,000 or so 'delivery executives' since they are technically contractors working with the company.[24] The progressive sheen of the initiative did little to make life better for those at the bottom of the pyramid.

To put it simply, in the gig economy, the game is rigged, and it will never enable those who execute the commands of its algorithms to break into vastly improved standards of living.

~

Insecure Employment

Government jobs will remain overwhelmingly popular among Indian millennials as long as the private sector is viewed as exploitative.

A clear example of exploitation can be seen in the introduction of the gig economy in India, when many drivers being lured to new platforms such as Uber were promised a better life and working conditions. Gautam Mody, Secretary of the New Trade Union Initiative, told The *Guardian* newspaper in 2018, 'The fact is that Uber created a perception that spread by word of mouth. I know not just of drivers who left OK jobs, but of office employees—lower-level accountants and bank clerks—who left their jobs to earn better money as Uber drivers.'[25] It wasn't just unskilled workers joining these platforms, but even salaried private sector employees lured by higher wages. This initial period, almost a gold rush for services provided by mobile applications, was underwritten by foreign capital flowing into India from companies based in places such as Japan, the United States and Saudi Arabia. Not only did these venture capital-backed unicorns throw enormous sums of money to acquire 'driver partners' and 'delivery executives', but also to attract customers.

But the tap had to stop flowing at some point, and many of these companies scaled their benefits back quickly.

Sunil Borkar, the leader of a Mumbai trade union which represents Uber drivers characterized their dire conditions, thus: 'Now they are saddled with car loans they can't pay off. Some are desperate, breaking their backs and just breaking even, if that. There is no exit for them.'

In a traditional workplace, if an employer is reducing pay, they usually announce it to its employees. But in the app economy, reduction in pay is determined by an opaque algorithm and often never communicated to the worker.

Due to high loans, expensive maintenance at authorized centres as well as low revenues per kilometre, many Uber drivers in places like Delhi often make less than auto rickshaw drivers. In March and October of 2018, Uber and Ola drivers participated in large strikes across the country protesting the decline in wages since the companies took off in 2013. Some claimed they were making Rs 200, or $3 a day.[26] With Uber's May 2019 Initial Public Offering (IPO) proving to be a disappointment, and at the time of writing, Ola laying the groundwork for its own IPO, the companies have aggressively sought ways to stem their losses and increase revenues. One of the first steps they took was to cut back on driver incentives and increase their own commissions.

This is a story which takes place around the world, but the stakes are much higher in a developing country like India, where men as young as twenty or twenty-one years of age are often married, and responsible for supporting not just their wives and children, but even their parents.

Although the government is rolling out national health insurance programs such as Ayushman Bharat, the uncertain and in many ways, exploitative, nature of the gig economy leaves millions of its members in a deep state of vulnerability. For example, if a delivery boy's bike gets stolen at work, who is liable? While researching this chapter, I found too many news reports of delivery boys who had been hit by vehicles or were injured at work and then faced long and arduous processes to get compensated, which was almost always a meagre sum.[27]

Even the manufacturing sector, long thought to be the most robust, leaves its workers in unstable employment and financial conditions. *IndiaSpend*, a data-driven journalism non-profit organization reported in March 2019 that companies across India were scaling back on hiring permanent employees in favour of contract workers, who are paid less and are easier to terminate.[28] *IndiaSpend*'s journalists interviewed protesting workers at Daikin India's plant in Alwar, Rajasthan, in the aftermath of clashes between workers and police in the industrial hub of Neemrana.[29]

They wrote about Premchand, a twenty-one-year-old contract worker from Haryana who was fired from his job after returning from his own wedding. Although he was hired back, the company made him 'rejoin', which meant that he was given a new worker identification number and his work history was wiped clean. He therefore had to settle for an entry-level salary, despite having worked with Daikin since 2014.

'I came back to the same production line doing the same job, but lost my previous work record,' Premchand said. He added: 'There has been only a Rs 1500 increment since I joined in 2014.'[30] He earned Rs 8200 a month before he was locked out of the factory for protesting. Others interviewed described how contract workers essentially performed identical functions as permanent workers, but for almost half the pay and without any extra benefits.

This is backed by data from the Indian Council for Research on International Economic Relations (ICRIER). The research centre found that employment grew by just six million in the organized industrial sector in the first fifteen years of the new millennium, from 7.7 million in 2000–2001 to 13.7 million jobs in 2015–2016, and that more than half of this increase was among contract workers. Thus, even as employment itself has slowed down, the proportion of contract workers has ballooned, together creating incredible instability at the micro- and macro-economic level.

According to an ICRIER report, 'These workers can be fired easily, have little or no job security and enjoy far fewer benefits in terms of health, safety, welfare and social security compared to directly employed workers. Given the deplorable conditions under which they work, a rapid increase of such jobs is unlikely to meet the challenge of productive job creation.'[31]

Young and millennial workers are in a no-win situation. If 'employed' in the gig economy, they largely struggle to make ends meet in an uncertain cycle of work, and if they're in manufacturing, they're often victims of industry-wide cost-cutting measures. Almost all of the employment being created in India today comprises low-end service jobs with scant prospects of upward mobility. The chances of rising up and making a living wage are limited if not impossible.

Technology, mobile applications and easy-to-use platforms have made life easier for the consumer or the end user and have generated revenues for the companies and venture capital funds which back them. However, they have failed to create prosperity for the millions who power these platforms. Faceless algorithms have become the new bosses, issuing instructions to millions through alerts and notifications.

All of which brings us back to the coveted government jobs, which not only offer lifetime employment and pensions, but provide a level of dignity missing in the private sector. India has long promised a move to the private sector as the definitive path towards greater wealth as a nation. Millennials are meant to be the generation leading that charge. However, the let-down of the gig economy and unstable nature of private employment has traumatized a generation, opening them up to vulnerability to a volatile future. A government job seems more attractive.

~

What's Different?

When I shared the insights from my field work with friends and family, they often remarked, 'India has always been like this,' and ask me, 'What makes millennials different?'

This is indeed one of the questions I kept in mind while writing this book: What truly makes millennials different? What makes their situation special when compared to previous generations or alternatively, what sets them apart from millennials from other countries?

In terms of professional and economic aspirations, it often feels like India has frozen in time. Young Indians today are no different from previous generations at a similar age. Yet, things are different for them.

India is no longer socialist, and the average Indian youth today is far more educated than in previous generations. Given the dire economic climate which began in the 2010s, this means that most jobs she is applying for are actually below her qualifications. Education is no longer the ticket to social mobility that it was promised to be.

Azim Premji University's 2018 State of Working India report found that the rate of unemployment among the educated has reached 16 per cent.[32] These numbers likely underestimated the actual unemployment rate given the prevalence of large-scale disguised unemployment across the economy and how most economic activity in India takes place in the informal sector.

But creating jobs is only one side of the coin. While full employment remains a distant dream, millennials will never be economically or personally satisfied if their employment does not match their educational qualifications. And due to the successes of education policies in creating millions of highly educated young Indians on paper, job opportunities rarely match the educational pedigree.

In summing up the bleak outlook for this set of millennials, ICRIER economist Radhicka Kapoor, told me, 'These are people whose parents have probably taken huge loans to send them to college. So they will probably end up doing things which they are overqualified to do, creating labour undervaluation in a qualitative sense,' she continued.[33]

I saw this first-hand at a job fair organized by the Delhi government in January 2019. It was a bone-chilling cold morning when I arrived at the Thyagraj Stadium, built a decade earlier, for the 2010 Commonwealth Games.

For two days in January, the Delhi government was using the stadium to hold a job fair, conceived to help youth in the capital region to find jobs.

I was alerted to this event by an advertisement in one of the big newspapers three days earlier. Chief Minister Arvind

Kejriwal's face occupied half the poster, and the other half crammed all the relevant details about the fair. I saved the clipping since I wanted to see the jobs available and talk to the job seekers.

The stadium was packed. Apart from employers, the crowd largely comprised young Indians, their parents and some college instructors. At the entrance was a large billboard with information about the companies present and the roles they were looking to fill.

I recognized very few companies. Among the big names, Ola Cabs was hiring 500 'driver partners', Patanjali, 100 marketing interns, Bikanervalaa, 100 each of shift managers, cashiers, counter boys and cooks, and G4S was hiring 600 security guards. The qualification for almost all of these roles was high school graduation. Then, there were lots of sales jobs on offer. From Indiabulls to Bandhan Bank, it appeared that many firms were looking for help with sales. But with a caveat. A majority of the sales positions were commission-based and not salaried. This meant that these agents would only get a cut from every product or service they sold, as opposed to a stable salary which would provide them with some degree of economic security. Classifying them as 'sales' employment in itself is a stretch, since most were actually tele-marketing.

I approached a group of friends who had come to the job fair together and started talking to them. There was a universal sense of disappointment, with most people unhappy that they couldn't find a 'computer' job. I then spoke with a thirty-something old teacher from the nearby Air Force Vocational College who had accompanied some of her students to help them find jobs. I thought it was a nice gesture for her to do so on a cold January morning, when she could have just stayed home. She was specifically looking out for data-management roles, since that was what her students were training for, but found that the few firms hiring IT professionals wanted them to either have a master's degree or significant work experience, even for positions which were actually entry-level.

'Can you believe they want five to seven years of work experience or a master's degree for a Rs 10,000 job?' she asked me, frustrated. I could believe it, given the deep employment crisis ravaging India, but sighed along with her in exasperation.

After queuing up at various company tables to ask them about their open positions, I struck up a conversation with a man about my age, whom I had seen in the same lines as me a few times throughout the morning. He was an electrical engineer who got his degree from Maharshi Dayanand University in Haryana. He was twenty-four and had come to the job fair as a last resort, after having looked for employment using traditional methods for two years. He wasn't short on money, since he had taken up seasonal work on short-term tenders for public projects in Rohtak but was keen on finding a well-paying and stable job. He discovered that the role that came closest to his qualifications was that of a sales representative at a solar power company. He didn't even bother asking the company for more information.

Baba Ramdev's Patanjali Ayurved appealed to the inner patriotism of those at the job fair, offering them a 'golden opportunity to contribute in nation building'. Intrigued by this unique pitch, I asked one of the recruiters from the godman's sprawling business empire for more information. He told me that they were only looking for marketing interns, who would be paid Rs 5000 a month to essentially go to kirana stores around Delhi and the NCR region and get them to stock Patanjali products. For this travel, there was a conveyance of

Rs 2000 a month, essentially elevating the salary to Rs 7000, an almost impossible sum to survive on whether you live alone or with family. Surprisingly or not, the Patanjali booth was among the least crowded.

The country's unemployment epidemic is not Arvind Kejriwal's fault, nor in his control. But the reality remains that there is a large number of urban youth armed with degrees and dreams failing to find employment opportunities commensurate to their aspirations. Millions of such stories exist within India.

~

Timepass

I have seen this play out in different versions across India. 850 kilometres from Delhi is Jabalpur, a once-prosperous industrial town in Madhya Pradesh, home to a government ordnance factory. In the 1950s and 60s, it was one of central India's most industrialized cities, home to a vibrant working class.

When I visited in 2018, I was surprised to find a city in decline. Travelling around Jabalpur's urban and exurban environs, I was struck by the number of young men everywhere—on the roadside, at public squares, outside shops and buildings—seemingly unemployed and disengaged from any economic activity.

Many of these young men came from agricultural families, but their aspirations lie elsewhere, not in farming.

Some experts and intellectuals have argued that formal employment is not the most common or useful form of work in rural India. Because of the seasonal nature of agriculture, holding a formal job makes it difficult to help out on the family farm during sowing and harvesting.

And some rural youth still see it this way. Many spend time in the cities near their homes when they are not needed to help out with farm work; however, they largely do so because there are no attractive work opportunities in their villages. Furthermore, the continued subdivision of rural landholdings has rendered farming almost unsustainable as a way to support a decent living.

The sight of young Indians loitering around town squares is not surprising to anyone who takes regular trips outside India's big cities, but the scale of unemployment in Jabalpur was really something else. Apart from the ongoing campaign for the state elections, there didn't seem to be any productive activity taking place. Australian academic Craig Jeffrey, while doing research in northwest Uttar Pradesh in the 2000s, studied this phenomenon and subsequently wrote a book about it, appropriately titled *Timepass*. In his research, Jeffrey focused on educated unemployed young men and rich farmers in and around Meerut to answer questions about class, politics and 'waiting'.[34]

During his fieldwork, Jeffrey 'met large numbers of unemployed young men in north India who were engaged in forms of waiting characterized by aimlessness and ennui. Unemployed young men in Meerut commonly spoke of being lost in time and they imagined many of their activities as simply ways to pass the time.'[35]

But what Jeffrey discovered was that it is was not uneducated, illiterate youth who were engaged in 'timepass'. Educated young men were, in fact, the biggest participants of the activity, though perhaps even the word 'participate' suggests a level of choice they did not have in the matter. They had not chosen this lifestyle voluntarily. As Jeffrey told me over email, 'a decline in the availability of public-sector employment and failure of economic growth to create graduate jobs was the primary cause. Allied to this, young people lacked some of the skills to start their own business and the infrastructural and institutional environment militated against entrepreneurship.'

He may as well have been describing the people I met in Jabalpur.

~

Pakora, inc.

I was in Jabalpur during the state's 2018 assembly elections, and although the purpose of my visit was to investigate how millennials intended to vote, I was more arrested by the lack of employment that seemed to prevail everywhere.

One evening, I had a few minutes before attending a *jansabha* organized by a Congress candidate, so I found myself at a *nashta ka dukaan*, or snack stall. It was around 6 p.m., and the sun was about to set. I ordered myself a cup of chai and looked around at the people gathered outside.

A group of friends, mostly men, but a few women as well, had arrived, and I started talking to them. They were all graduates of the Rani Durgavati Vishwavidyalaya, also known as the University of Jabalpur, which was considered among the better institutions in town.

Strikingly, not a single one of them was formally employed.

'We all did our graduation in engineering. But there are no engineering jobs here for us. We will have to move elsewhere to find employment,' one of the men in the group told me.

There's a popular adage which describes engineering education in India: You become an engineer first, and then figure out what to do with your life.

This was playing out in front of my eyes in Jabalpur. The people at the snack stall had all gone to decent colleges, but elsewhere, I met as many engineers who got their degrees from nondescript two-room engineering colleges in crowded marketplaces. When I went to one of these colleges, I met a teacher who told me he was only teaching students because he had been rejected from every other job he had applied for.

Thirty years ago, many of the families of these young people did not have a stable income nor access to twenty-four-hour electricity supply. Some didn't even have pucca houses. Today, they have most of that, but vibrant employment opportunities are scarce. Gauging from their responses, it was clear that many of these individuals were just about surviving, far from thriving.

A twenty-five-year-old man in the group told me about having to ask his parents for permission to travel to Bhopal, five hours away by train. 'I only have money to buy snacks. I can watch movies at the cinema hall occasionally. For most other things, I have to ask my parents for cash.'

A man of his age and qualification should not just have a stable job and enough financial liquidity to purchase his own train ticket, but also possess the agency to make his own decisions, which comes with economic security.

'Educated unemployment' is therefore a crisis that defines millennials more than any other demographic group in the country. In January 2018, Prime Minister Modi sat down for a televised interview with ZEE News anchor Sudhir Chaudhary. In response to a question about the job crisis in India, Modi asked his interviewer: 'If a man selling pakoras outside the Zee TV office takes home Rs 200 at the end of the day, is that not employment?'

Modi, a measured and calculated speaker, was completely off the mark, and in response, the Congress Party said that if frying pakoras is classified as employment, begging should be included as well.

Modi's answer was obviously disrespectful towards India's aspirational and educated millennials, but also more alarmingly made clear that India's so-called 'demographic dividend' could become a demographic disaster if not treated correctly. If the leader of the nation believes that frying food for Rs 200 daily qualifies as the sort of employment the country ought to create for its youth, it will never break out of poverty.

And that's because the math simply doesn't add up. If a young Indian man were to open a stall frying pakoras and make Rs 200 a day working every single day, he would make Rs 6000 a month.

That doesn't even include his operating costs. Even if it did, and he made Rs 6000 in absolute profit, that would still not be enough to survive, let alone thrive, in modern India. It is simply not sufficient for a single man, even if he lives with his parents, and it is certainly not enough to support a wife and children.

~

One evening towards the end of my stay in Jabalpur, I found myself back at the snack stall, talking to its owner, Radhe, a thirty-two-year-old civil engineer and first-generation graduate. After he was laid off from a construction company in 2015, no one was willing to hire him, and he could not move elsewhere because he had to look after his ailing parents. So, he set up a stall, where he sold pakoras, kachoris and tea. After expenses, he brought home about Rs 5000 every month. His wife, a librarian at a private school, made Rs 12,000, which was how the family primarily sustained itself.

'Being an engineer doesn't mean much. I wish I had applied for a government job instead. I would have at least had a stable income and been able to provide for my family,' he told me.

His wife was an anomaly, given women's participation in the workforce has fallen sharply since 2000. A World Bank study found that nearly 20 million women dropped out of the workforce between 2004 and 2012, and a Tata Sons-Dalberg analysis estimated that approximately 120 million women in India have a secondary education but do not participate in the workforce.[36] Radhe's wife, Nandini, worked because her husband didn't make enough. Her situation suggested that women's involvement in the labour force could save families from destitution. The Tata-Dalberg study further found that women's employment could add Rs 31 trillion rupees, or roughly $440 billion, to India's GDP, but a variety of structural inequities prevented women from joining the workforce: from existing social taboo and gender norms to safety and mobility.

The idea of self-reflective and anxious millennials is something of a trope used to mischaracterize the generation. But real financial and economic anxiety exists among millennials, particularly those who have to support their families and find or maintain stable employment. With more than 120 million women missing from the workforce and a lack of vibrant economic opportunities, young couples in the millennial bracket don't only struggle to fulfil their dreams, but quite literally to put two meals on the table.

The United Nations Development Programme estimates that India needs to create nearly 300 million jobs between 2015 and 2050 to capitalize on its demographic dividend.[37] But these jobs cannot include frying snacks by the road or begging. They must be generated in labour intensive and stable sectors of the economy, largely in the formal manufacturing sector.

The bleak reality is that millennials are stuck in a low wage trap. Either they have employment which is low-paying or unpredictable, or they have no jobs at all. The resulting economic insecurity has and will continue to have profound effects on the future of the country and the social attitudes of millennials.

It appears grimly inevitable that the countless years of lost or wasted economic output for millions of young Indians will have significant repercussions in the decades to come. Most millennials are at a point in their lives where they need stable employment and economic security. Older and younger millennials have families to support. In a 21st Century economy where the very nature of work changes every couple of years, this is the most crucial period in the careers of millennials to establish themselves and attain economic security. Else, its most promising generation on paper will rely on the state for incentives and schemes instead of putting money back into society and creating growth.

~

Startup India

There is a growing number of Indian millennials who are challenging the status quo and becoming entrepreneurs.

After having spent six months as an apprentice at a bean-to-bar chocolate brand based in Mysore, Shambhavi Sahai was on her next venture. When I interviewed her for the book in June 2019, she was in the process of expanding her made-to-order smoothie business while also working as a fashion stylist.

Shambhavi is not an average Indian millennial. She went to one of India's best schools, the Shri Ram School in Gurgaon, until her final two years, which she completed at a boarding school in Connecticut. She then got a degree in International Relations and Economics from a top-ranked liberal arts college in the United States, interning in South Africa and New York City during her summer breaks.

With a fancy degree and education in hand, Shambhavi could have chosen to work anywhere in the world. But she returned to India after graduating to tap into the country's massively expanding appetite for consumption.

'Options in the US for me, particularly because I would have been on a visa, were limited and not the best,' she said. 'Meanwhile, the opportunities in India are huge. There's a huge growth rate in the technology and F&B space.'

She continued: 'The opportunities here are also very interesting. You can either create them or search for them. There's a lot of room to create opportunities for yourself and others.'

After moving back home, she explored jobs at small businesses and start-ups to learn the ropes of starting a business in India. This was how she came across Earth Loaf, an artisanal chocolate company, on Instagram. A friend had gifted her some of their chocolate, and she soon decided she would work at the company to understand how artisanal chocolate was made.

'I wanted to work at a sustainable business which hires local people. Additionally, because I am vegan, I like to understand where my food comes from, and Earth Loaf is a bean-to-bar company.'

So she sent them a direct message on Instagram and soon found herself with an opportunity to work as an apprentice at their factory in Mysore.

'India is still very network-based. I have gotten all my internships and jobs so far by just messaging people, mostly on Instagram.'

Earth Loaf was founded by David Belo and Angelika Anagnostou, South African entrepreneurs who spent their careers in the F&B business in Europe before deciding to make and sell chocolate in India. At Earth Loaf, Shambhavi took on a variety of roles, from representing the company at sales fairs to serving as a taster.

Earth Loaf (which has since rebranded to Naviluna) has a specific sort of customer. Targeted largely at millennials and working professionals, the company sells its chocolates through tie-ups with cafes. Their business plan involves selling their chocolate to people who would spend approximately Rs 200 on a cup of coffee, a vibrant segment of the market given the rapid expansion of coffee shops, large and small, across India's metropolitan cities.

Shambhavi had a great time working for the company, and decided she wanted to continue in the consumer goods space. She moved back home to Delhi to work at another start-up, Stage3, an Indian version of the American designer wear rental platform, Rent the Runway. At Stage3, she conducted due diligence for investors, created content, and helped the marketing team to run regressions on their target customers and their spending habits.

But Shambhavi knew she wanted to do her own thing. Working for others was great, but she would learn the most on her own, making her own mistakes.

She decided to start making smoothies from her kitchen. Since she had recently adopted a vegan lifestyle, smoothies were new additions to her diet, and because she was making them for herself, she decided to explore a business opportunity in making and selling them to others.

'Most of my customers are from my personal network or Instagram,' Shambhavi told me. 'I have had a lot of people find me through Instagram, and my clients are largely working professionals, lawyers or doctors in Gurgaon or South Delhi.'

She continued: 'They are a mix between people who are interested in vegan or healthy lifestyles, and those who just like smoothies for their taste.'

As India's wealthy continue to amass more economic power, the opportunities to provide them goods and services are endless. From renting designer clothes to selling artisanal chocolate, there is significant room to expand when your clientele is in South Delhi or South Mumbai. This is a segment of the market which has made its money in India but travels abroad extensively. These people want the products and experiences available abroad in India.

Priyanka Kanwar's story is not very different from Shambhavi's. After graduating from Yale University, with experience in consulting and microfinance through internships, Kanwar decided to found Kite, a payments platform to simplify cash transactions in India.

'I started Kite because I have always been very intrigued by the access to finance in India,' Priyanka told me. 'Most people are left completely out of the financial system or don't have access to it. So, when I came back from college, in the five years I had stayed out of India, a lot of things had changed: millions had smartphones in their hands and data had become extremely cheap. Therefore, the opportunity to increase access to financial services through apps could have become a reality.'

But it was a huge challenge to make Kite's first product a success. Due to the Reserve Bank of India's flurry of constantly changing regulations and intense competition from companies such as PayTM, PhonePe, Google Pay and Amazon Pay, and a high cash burn rate, it became clear that merely processing payments would not be a sustainable business model. 'Even though we had millions of users signing onto the platform, consumers in India are very fickle. We could not collect enough data points on them,' Priyanka added.

So she changed her product entirely, moving from the consumer to the business side, creating a technology-driven credit card platform for small and medium enterprises (SMEs). 'We have partnered with some of the biggest banks in India, but despite having access to everything, these banks have not been able to innovate on products. We therefore offer SMEs a wide range of products and tools through our platform, from filing GST returns to recording and tracking employee expenditures.'

I visited the Kite office in 2018. Situated in Delhi's Okhla industrial area, it felt like it could have been anywhere in Silicon Valley. There were no office cabins, but an open floor plan where team members went about from desk to desk working on projects collaboratively. I was welcomed by Adam, an American classmate of Kanwar's from Yale, who was working as Kite's chief of staff. He was a South Asian Studies major and seemed to have a fairly philosophical take on India which made for interesting, yet at-times puzzling conversation.

There's something to be said about the impatience of millennial founders. I asked Priyanka why she wanted to start her own venture right after graduation instead of working elsewhere. Her response was pretty straightforward. 'I always knew I wanted to become an entrepreneur, and I realized the fastest way to learn is to jump right into it. What I have learned in the last one or two years, I wouldn't have learned in ten or fifteen years elsewhere.'

Her business partner, Prabhtej Singh Bhatia, was featured in GQ Magazine's 2018 list of '50 Most Influential Young Indians' for launching Simba, a craft beer which has been introduced in Goa and other Indian cities. The beer is brewed in Chhattisgarh, where his family has an existing alcohol business. He divides his time and attention between Kite and Simba. Prabhtej also spent time abroad, getting an undergraduate degree in economics from the University of Exeter and was Priyanka's school friend. In fact, they began discussing plans to start a business together right when they were in school. Kite was Priyanka's passion project. She had taken a gap year before Yale to intern with Muhammad Yunus' Grameen Foundation and wanted to increase access to the formal banking sector for those outside of it. Prabhtej was determined to take his family's business empire, which stretched from construction to liquor, into the 21st Century. After observing the craft beer culture in England when he was a student there, he decided to add it to his family's existing portfolio.

India, with its arcane alcohol regulations which vary from state to state, is a regulatory nightmare for would-be liquor entrepreneurs. Just the costs to navigate regulations can balloon to dozens of lakhs of rupees every year. In many states, the government is the only liquor distributor, so developing connections with the responsible officials can be a skill (backed up by the necessary capital) of its own. In addition to the access to capital, Prabhtej therefore had an invaluable advantage when launching Simba: industry 'know-how'.

~

In 2020, millennials formed approximately half of the global workforce.[38] A PricewaterhouseCoopers survey of more than 4000 millennials from around the world found that 'millennials tend to be uncomfortable with rigid corporate structure and turned off by information silos. They expect rapid progression, a varied and interesting career and constant feedback.'[39] India's professional millennials are no different. Shambhavi, Priyanka and Prabhtej are all among a group of young Indians with global education. From well-to-do families, the aspirations and stories of these young Indians should not be dismissed due to their small numbers, but understood because of their impact, presently and potentially, on India's economic and political systems.

Entrepreneurs Bhavish Aggarwal and Ritesh Agarwal, no relation to each other, dominate newspaper headlines for being among the youngest self-made billionaires in the country. The respect and admiration they command is only parallel to the kind Narayana Murthy and his Infosys co-founders commanded when they began their venture in the 1980s.

After finishing his engineering degree at IIT Bombay, Bhavish worked at Microsoft for two years before quitting in 2010. When he told his father about his plan to start a taxi-aggregating service with his engineering classmate, his father was puzzled. 'Kya beta IIT karke travel agency kholna hai!' (You finished IIT just to start a travel agency?)[40]

In his own words, Bhavish had a 'very middle-class upbringing'. But he had a degree from one of India's top institutions and he was restless to do more. 'We didn't have any money, we didn't have capital, but we powered on,' he said. 'I think a grounded beginning helps you build things for the long-term. Our humble beginnings helped us keep our head down and focus on the essentials: consumers and a good financial system.'

Ola is now one of two big players in India's taxi rental space, along with Uber. It has raised billions of dollars from investors around the world, including SoftBank, which also owns a large stake in its rival, Uber. But Ola didn't quite begin precisely as a rival to Uber or its business model. It began as olatrips.com to help users book taxis for out-of-town journeys.[41] But not too many people were buying these trips. After experimenting with car rentals, Aggarwal and his co-founder realized the real problem to be solved was travel within cities. They set up the service, even personally driving customers who called them on their phones. They later launched their smartphone application, and once they received funding of $5 million from Tiger Global Management, an American hedge fund, they realized they were on to something big.[42]

After that, there was no looking back. At the time of writing this, Ola was operating taxis in more than 150 Indian cities, aggressively expanding in Australia and England, and entering the electric vehicle space, about to break ground on an approximately Rs 2000 crore factory in Tamil Nadu to manufacture 10 million electric scooters a year.[43]

Bhavish could have probably stayed with Microsoft, gotten promoted a few times before most likely getting an MBA at a top-rated American institution, and found himself making hundreds of thousands of dollars in Silicon Valley or Seattle, just like so many IIT engineers.

But he chose to give all that up in pursuit of something unpredictable. Uber had not taken off yet, and Ola's success was dependent on a wide range of external factors. Millennials are often lampooned for being irresponsible or reckless when making important decisions. But such decisions occasionally lead to monumental payoffs, as in Aggarwal's case.

Ritesh Agarwal took an even bigger risk. He was enrolled in the University of London's International Programme provided by the Indian School of Business and Finance in Delhi, 'to keep [his] parents happy'.[44] But he knew he wanted to be an entrepreneur, so he dropped out and applied for a $100,000 fellowship and the chance to be mentored by PayPal founder Peter Thiel, specifically for founders under the age of twenty who drop out of college. He was accepted in 2013, at the age of 18, and went on to found OYO Rooms, an aggregator of budget hotel rooms which has become India's largest hospitality chain.

Valued at $10 billion in 2020, Agarwal has set his sights beyond India, having embarked on an aggressive expansion in China. Between 2017 and 2020, he claims to have signed up more than 19,000 hotels in the country to offer customers 900,000 rooms in 338 Chinese cities.[45] Agarwal claims it has become the world's third largest hotel chain, behind only Marriott International and Hilton Worldwide, and is on track to surpass its competitors in 2023.[46] Just like Ola, OYO's ambitions are not limited to India. The world is truly an oyster for these millennial entrepreneurs.

Agarwal doesn't come from an exceptionally wealthy or well-connected family. His father used to run a small business in the town of Bissamcuttack in Odisha, and his mother is a homemaker.[47] But he had fire in his belly. When he walked into a meeting with Venture Capitalist Bejul Somaia in 2014, the investor was most interested in Agarwal's backpack, which looked heavy.[48] Somaia asked the teenager what was in it and was struck by the answer. Agarwal was carrying all his belongings with him since he was changing rooms and hotels every night. He knew the struggle it took to succeed, and more importantly, he knew the challenge he needed to solve as a start-up founder.

Disruption can come from the unlikeliest of places. Some of the people mentioned here will succeed, and others may fail. But their stories are important because they represent a new generation of young Indians who aren't looking to use their education or privilege to build careers outside of India. They are hungry to capitalize on the millions of potential customers within the country. Without a doubt, they will form the top ranks of millennial leaders who will hold the levers of social, economic and political power in the years to come.

These people are among those who are actually creating millions of jobs in the country, even though many of these jobs are in the unstable, shifting gig economy. Bhavish Aggarwal's Ola, in fact, is one of the companies which forms the bedrock of India's gig economy. He is now venturing into electric vehicles and could very well help power a new, much-needed industry in the country and create thousands of new jobs. Ritesh Agarwal's OYO has become the go-to hotel chain for those visiting small town India and for budget travellers.

For a real Silicon Valley to take off in India it is important for the country to create and nurture talent locally. Priyanka Kanwar and Prabhtej Bhatia are doing that on a smaller scale. Kite employs a diverse team of millennials, from theologists to technical engineers, to create new financial products where Indian banks are lagging on innovating.

Yes, these people are among a few who have made the economy work for them, but their kinds of aspirations are shared by millions of urban, middle class young Indians, many of whom nurture similar dreams. A study by the National Association of Software and Service Companies found that Indian entrepreneurs founded more than 1200 new start-ups in 2018, mostly in the technology sector, creating 40,000 new jobs directly, and roughly 100,000 indirectly.[49] Almost half of this growth came from outside India's biggest cities, in places like Kerala, Jaipur, and Chandigarh. There are now more than 50,000 start-ups in India, and private equity deal volume among start-ups was estimated at 26.3 billion US dollars in 2018.[50]

These start-ups are in areas such as enterprise solutions FinTech, EdTech, HealthTech, and have quickly become ubiquitous in the country. Apart from Ola and OYO, you have probably had a doctor's appointment scheduled on Practo, a health technology start-up founded by Shashank ND and Abhinav Lal, when they were both college students in 2008. Or you have ordered food on Swiggy, which became India's fastest unicorn, valued at a billion dollars four years after it was founded by BITS Pilani alumni in their twenties.

The list continues, but the point is that there's a section of young Indians unafraid to take certain risks in hopes of hitting it big. This is unique to new India. In the old India, a thirty-year-old becoming a billionaire through a self-started business in a matter of a few years was not just rare, it was simply impossible.

~

For India to succeed, take advantage of the 21st Century and become an economic powerhouse, the country will not only need to create millions of blue-collar manufacturing jobs but also many more homegrown start-ups to succeed like Ola and OYO.

But even though technology provides opportunity, it also deepens anxiety. The internet and social media have made jobless youth in smaller towns aware of their counterparts in Gurgaon and Bandra Kurla Complex working for banks and consulting firms. Unemployable engineers know about their brethren at IITs and Infosys and are trying to figure out how some got the golden ticket while they didn't. None of these problems are unique to India. But the growing income inequality and the lack of a new sunrise industry like IT in the

1990s and early 2000s has made it nearly impossible for the expansion or deepening of a new middle class.

The number of those with unmet aspirations and lost opportunities is only rising. T.V. Mohandas Pai, former Infosys executive and chairman of Manipal University, is a regular cheerleader of the BJP on social media and one of Modi's biggest evangelists. In 2014, he made a rough calculation of the number of jobless youth in the country. 'Of the 25 million babies born every year, one million don't reach the age of twenty-one and mostly die before the age of 5. Of the [remaining] 24 million, 30 per cent may go into agriculture or drop out. Of these 17 million, 10 million are not getting decent jobs or earning decent wages. For the last 10 years, this amounts to 100 million people. So, we have 100 million people in the age group of 21 to 35 all over India with no good jobs.'[51]

Although I could not independently verify his numbers, they are within the realm of reality. And the underbelly of joblessness is economic insecurity, which leaves millennials in a state of constant financial anxiety. Strikingly, roughly 10 per cent of the millennials I interviewed for my book lived on their own. And almost all those who lived away from their parents were migrants.

In many western, as well as Asian cultures, living at home after finishing college is considered unusual. This is largely because most young adults crave their independence and do not want family watching over them. Further, they have their jobs to support themselves.

In India, the opposite is true. For one, it is often considered taboo to not live with your parents—some may even get offended if their children choose to live apart. But many adults live at home purely out of necessity. Low earnings and the high cost of home ownership have made renting and buying property very difficult for millennials.

But the sense of lost opportunity and unfulfilled aspirations is much deeper and wider. And it was more common among the older millennials I interviewed over the course of my research.

I found that a large cohort of older millennials—those born between 1982 and 1988, roughly aged between thirty and thirty-six when I met them—felt that they had already missed the boat. Many of them were not optimistic about the future. Most were in precarious financial positions, juggling high household expenditures along with school fees, which induced severe anxiety about unforeseen events that could affect their economic well-being—the health of their parents, family problems and even road accidents. The CSDS study found that these anxieties were almost universal across Indian youth today: 91 per cent of youth in big cities said they were anxious about their parents' health, while 88 and 85 per cent of those in smaller cities and villages said the same.

Similarly, 88 per cent of youth in big cities said they were anxious about their own health and 77 per cent said they were anxious about their jobs and employment.[52]

CSDS asked its respondents fourteen questions to construct an 'Index of Anxiety' – which investigated their worries about issues such as employment, education, personal health, parents' health and even mob violence. These responses were then used to categorize the responses of those surveyed.

And remarkably, the CSDS study found that the more educated a young person is, the more anxious she becomes. Among those who had graduate degrees and above, 64 per cent were found to be 'highly anxious', and another 23 per cent were 'somewhat anxious'. For high school graduates, these numbers were 50 and 28 per cent respectively.

It is not hard to understand why better educated millennials are more anxious. The economy is simply not creating enough jobs for educated Indians. These people were promised a better life in return for their hard work, degrees and qualifications but reality was starkly different.

India's 1991 liberalization did not immediately transform the economy in the way many thought it would. It most significantly benefited those who were best positioned to take advantage of the inflow of capital and new opportunities: the urban, well-educated elite. This elite no longer needed to send their children to medical colleges or prepare them for the UPSC. The children of this elite now dominate India's private sector, having benefited from crucial networks of caste and class to help them take advantage of new opportunities.

But with liberalization also came stagnation and great uncertainty. The once-vibrant factory towns like Jabalpur have become living museums of stagnation and decline. New opportunities presented themselves, but they came with great uncertainty, such as the gig economy—where drivers and delivery 'executives' are unable to hoist themselves into financial stability and economic security.

But one prevailing sentiment unites millennials of all backgrounds across the country—economic insecurity. A combination of jobless growth, sharp annual increases in the cost of living, a rapidly globalizing world, and global economic trends which favour robots and algorithms over real people has consigned India's millennials to severe economic insecurity and anxiety. Unfortunately, Indian millennials today are fighting from the back foot, always on the defensive. Numerous external and internal challenges are keeping the generation stuck in a vicious cycle, binding them from moving to the front foot to embrace their ambitions and potential and make the most of the 21st Century.

Indian millennials could have two very different experiences: one for the top 1 per cent, which uses its networks of power and privilege to profit handsomely from globalization and any macroeconomic progress taking place in the country, and then another for the rest of the population, which will continue to fight for government jobs. These government jobs are the only opportunities that provide young Indians stability in an otherwise unstable and volatile job market. Job creation must therefore become a single-focus obsession of India's lawmakers.

Few other countries see as much discussion about their internal demographics as India. That's because India has one of the world's youngest populations. At the dawn of the new millennium, this was seen as India's biggest strength. It was felt that after the opening of the economy and the incredible growth of the IT industry, India's youth would make the country a 21st Century economic and technological superpower. But two decades in, the promise of this demographic advantage is fading.

TECHNOLOGY AND SOCIAL MEDIA

It's hard to get on an airplane in India without encountering at least ten people busy taking selfies. At Hyderabad airport in 2018, I noticed a fellow millennial taking more than fifty selfies from check-in to boarding. I stopped counting after that. A cool pout at the security line, a dashing Bollywood pose at the aerobridge, a seductive smile on seat 34D—no moment was too small for this excited young traveller.

In 2013, Oxford Dictionary, the undoubted guardian of the English language, named 'selfie' its word of the year, defining it as 'a photograph that one has taken of oneself, typically one taken with a smartphone or webcam and uploaded to a social media website.'[1] It beat out binge-watch, bitcoin, schmeat and twerk to claim the title, and with good reason: Research found that its frequency in the English language had increased by 17,000 per cent that year.[2] As smartphones with dual cameras became increasingly popular around the world, and internet and social media proliferated across the globe, millions took and uploaded photos of themselves to share with their social networks (there were over 23 million photos with the hashtag selfie uploaded on Instagram in 2013).[3]

At the time, many of these young people taking selfies were dismissed as vain or silly. Some went further, calling millennials narcissistic for their selfie habits. But in the Indian context, it is important to recognize the much larger phenomenon at play. Selfies, and social media platforms where they are uploaded, get young Indians to do something incredibly powerful and new— define themselves on their own terms.

In taking these photos, choosing the right angles, filters, and backdrops, and then uploading them to social media platforms or sending them to friends, millennials are in control of how they present themselves to the world. Technology and social media platforms have become powerful tools of self-expression in a conservative society, where elders and the patriarchy have for long wielded outsized influence on younger generations.

Further, something that was routine to me—travelling on an airplane—was not routine for millions joining India's middle class. Documenting these experiences through selfies, are a way for these individuals to demonstrate their newfound economic clout to their social networks. Therefore, this ability to define oneself on one's own terms is what defines millennials more than any other generation in India today.

•————•

Breaking Barriers through the Internet

Nazneen was twenty-six when she got married. Before that, she lived at home with her parents in Hyderabad and was the last unmarried girl in her neighbourhood.

Nazneen was from a middle-class family. Her father worked at a bank and her mother was a housewife. Her parents were neither liberal nor conservative. They didn't have strict rules for her growing up, but they expected her to marry a boy of their choice. And they were feeling the pressure. Their friends and family were beginning to ask why Nazneen was still unmarried and speculated that she might have a boyfriend—considered taboo in her society.

They decided to act fast and began looking for men for their daughter. They worried that it would get harder as she grew older, and that if they waited any longer, they would be left scraping the bottom of the barrel.

Then came good news: Nazneen's sister had found someone for her.

She first brought the match—a cousin of a friend of her husband's—to her parents. He was eight years older than Nazneen and was an aircraft engineer based in Qatar. He had a well-paying job and came from a good family, so they were excited and went ahead.

Nazneen was unwilling. She wanted to continue working at the call centre where she made good money, and with which she bought things that she had dreamed of owning while growing up. But her sister and the rest of her family told her that her fiancé earned well enough to take care of her and give her a comfortable life. They didn't understand what more she could want. 'If you wait any longer, there won't be anyone left for you,' they told her. 'You'll have to settle for a forty-year-old divorcee.'

Under this pressure, she gave in and agreed to the marriage. She met her fiancé twice before the nikah. She didn't particularly like or dislike him. She had very little in common with him, but her friends and family told her she needed to give it time before a bond grew between them.

Like millions of Indian families, her parents took credit from a local moneylender to finance her wedding, a lavish three-day event which culminated in a nikah.

A week after the wedding she moved with her husband to Doha, where she was expected to run their home and take care of him. To her shock, her husband would lock the house door from the outside as he left for work. He claimed this was in the interest of her safety. He would take her out on weekends, usually to a café or shopping mall, but rarely made conversation with her. Although she felt constrained, getting used to running her own home kept her busy for the first month.

Then the emotional abuse began. Nazneen's husband would return home well after midnight almost three nights a week, drunk and belligerent. After a few weeks, she began to suspect that he was having an affair and confronted him about it.

'I could smell cheap perfume on him. It reminded me of the *attar* girls doused on themselves back home in Hyderabad. It was rare for men to use it.'

True to form, he was drunk at the time of the conversation, and denied her accusations. To prove his point, he slapped her and made her sleep on the sofa in their living room from that day on. Every other week, he would demand she sleep in his bed, where he would rape her. That was just the beginning.

Her physical and sexual abuse continued for ten months, until Nazneen decided she couldn't take it anymore. She considered escaping, but her husband had confiscated her passport. She managed to find the phone number for the Indian embassy in Doha. She called it from a phone owned by another Indian housewife in her building, borrowing it one evening while taking the trash out of her apartment.

The embassy stepped in and helped her escape from Doha. But she was two months pregnant.

Returning home to Hyderabad pregnant and penniless, Nazneen thought her life was finished. She decided she would have her baby and figure things out afterwards. She knew she wouldn't have to worry about her parents pressuring her to get married again.

~

One day, four months into her pregnancy, Nazneen was scrolling through YouTube when a video caught her eye. It was a make-up tutorial. In these tutorials, women film themselves applying make-up while giving viewers tips on how to get the looks they want. Such videos have become a cottage industry in themselves, helping people of all colours and skin tones with finding and applying the right make-up.

She clicked on the video—she doesn't remember the name of the first expert she saw, but the tutorial stuck with her because it was an Indian woman talking in Hindi. In minutes, Nazneen became an addict.

'She told people like me what to do with make-up. Before her and the other videos, I used to look like a ghost,' Nazneen told me.

Nazneen estimates that she watched weeks' worth of make-up tutorials during her pregnancy and practised the techniques she learnt. Given the time she spent on the videos, it wasn't a surprise that she soon became an expert in make-up.

Through this time, even after she gave birth to her son in January 2017, Nazneen survived on pocket money from her parents, who were still paying off the loan they took for her wedding. She wanted to increase her limited spending power. She didn't just want to scrape by; she wanted to send her son to the best school available and give him a comfortable life, comparable to the one his father might have provided.

But how would she get there? Her degree in history didn't give her too many options. The only other thing she really knew was to apply make-up.

Nazneen got onto Facebook and WhatsApp, and reached out to her friends, neighbours, relatives, and their friends, offering her services as a make-up and nail artist. Soon, she began meeting clients, operating out of her parents' living room—they didn't have much of a problem with this set-up.

Before long, the living room at her parents' house became a beauty parlour and she expanded from make-up and nails to hair.

'I didn't charge much initially,' she told me. 'Most of my services were for around 150 rupees, and my costs weren't high. Since most of my clients were friends or relatives, I did not feel comfortable charging more.' Because she wasn't paying rent, Nazneen could afford to keep her prices low and still save more than enough to reinvest into providing more services.

A year after she began this work, she hired her first employee: another single mother in her neighbourhood. She was responsible for the easier tasks, such as billing, washing hair, and preparing hair dyes and face masks, while Nazneen would take on the more complex work.

And the payoff of that valuable work continued to increase: When I first met Nazneen in May 2019, she was in the process of opening her own salon, just off the highway from Hyderabad airport into the city, employing a staff of five.

'I had saved a lot of money from operating in my parents' home, but there wasn't enough space and the neighbours were complaining,' she said. 'It soon came to a point where I just knew I had to expand.'

She went on: 'All of my initial clients stayed with me. They then told their friends and relatives about me, and I got so many customers I had to start taking appointments.' She doesn't just support herself and her son, but even contributes money towards her parents' household expenses.

If the first part of Nazneen's story had unfolded as it did ten or twenty years earlier, she may not have been able to turn adversity into opportunity or to have so stunningly reversed her own fortune. No doubt, Nazneen is a remarkable woman, but she was able to do what she did because she had something that previous generations of remarkable young women didn't have. The internet.

From finding clients through Facebook and WhatsApp, to learning from influencers how to retain them, she didn't just use new resources available to her, but also capitalized on a radical change transforming India today. That change is the disruption caused by digital technology, the internet and social media.

~

Smartphones and social media give young Indians the ability to define themselves outside traditional frameworks and systems of identity, and millions of them are using this technology to write their own destinies.

There's a perception that millennials are addicted to social media. That they can't get off Facebook, Instagram, or WhatsApp. And in many ways, it is true. But what gets forgotten is that an entire generation in India today has been empowered by these digital communities. Nazneen's entire life had been mapped out for her, like for millions of other young Indians. She would go to school, go to college, get married, and start a family.

That all changed when the violence began. When Nazneen walked out, she decided that she was not going to be another victim of domestic abuse. Later, she decided she wasn't going to live off her parents either.

Nazneen had the courage to leave an abusive marriage. No one in her life thought she would start a beauty salon, and no one knew how to help her either. But the internet did. YouTube became her teacher, and Facebook and WhatsApp became her 'word of mouth'.

Millennials still hold onto old narratives—Nazneen did, after all, first get married to the person her parents chose. 'Elders always know best' is one of the key philosophies of Indian society. Many believe that young people should listen to their parents and follow the plans made for them, and that these plans will eventually lead them to comfortable lives. Making independent decisions is risky, largely because it involves embracing the unknown (what if that decision leads to failure?), but also because it upends existing systems of respect and power. As a result, many young Indians today continue to abide by decisions—economic, social and political—that others have made for them. Whether it is to study for the UPSC, or marry the person chosen by their family, these decisions are taken because they are safe.

In many cases, the internet only deepens existing narratives—it's not as though Facebook is a bastion of liberals. But the internet is also home to many other, more progressive narratives. Even if your father doesn't think you could start your own beauty business, you may find someone on the internet who believes you can.

There's been an almost entirely new field of analysis on the 'fourth industrial revolution' and how technology is set to change the very nature of work, value and opportunity. It seems increasingly likely that artificial intelligence and machine learning are going to render millions jobless and force them to completely restart their lives. This is particularly true of many industrialized economies. But for millennials in India, technology is leading to widespread social disruption. It is slowly breaking the bonds of age-old traditions, systems of power, and ways of life, and creating a generation that is more assertive of its own identity and beliefs.

The form that identity takes is shaped by the internet, too.

~

India's smartphone and data revolution is well-documented. It is the reason for the most important differentiator between millennials and previous generations: the access to information. Forty years ago, if you lived in a smaller town or village, your only access to big-city life or the outside world was a newspaper. In 2020, smartphones are available for as little as Rs 5000. Further, when Mukesh Ambani entered the telecommunications sector with Jio, the company slashed the price of mobile data, rapidly accelerating internet penetration in India. Thus, today, millennials anywhere in the country are able to connect to the internet and access the world through it. The majority of these millennials are not well-connected elites of Delhi or Mumbai, but belong to India's new middle class, not just in its big cities, but also its rapidly urbanizing smaller towns and villages.

These young Indians who couldn't afford the outrageously-priced iPhones when they began to be imported from the United States, can now choose from inexpensive Chinese-made smartphones which give them features almost identical to those of an iPhone. They don't need to travel to America to partake in its culture—they have it on their fingertips. Consider, for example, the millennial farmers in Telangana who went viral after filming their own version of American rapper Drake's 'Kiki challenge' on their paddy field with their bullocks and uploading their video on Instagram and YouTube.[4]

As of April 2019, YouTube had 265 million users in India.[5] This subscriber base was one of the main reasons why in October 2018, T-Series, a Bollywood music label and movie studio, dethroned PewDiePie, a Swedish gamer and comedian, to become YouTube's most-subscribed channel. Similarly, India is WhatsApp's biggest user base. Almost 400 million WhatsApp users are from India, one of the main reasons Facebook bought the app for $19 billion in 2014 when it was looking to dominate India's emerging social media and e-commerce platforms. In 2018, WhatsApp began piloting digital payments in India, and in 2020 Facebook announced a nearly $6 billion investment in Jio, with the hope of using WhatsApp as a building block for Jio's nascent e-commerce platform and facilitating its transactions.[6]

Since 2010, a truly unprecedented proliferation of technology and the internet has transformed India. The internet is no longer a playground reserved for the rich. Young people are no longer limited by their incomes or geographies—they can access the entire world without moving a kilometre. And what this revolution brought with it were incredible aspirations. That young people, if they worked hard, could unlock any doors they wanted to.

~

Santosh Desai, a social commentator and managing director for the brand consultancy Future Brands, told me that young Indians previously saw themselves as a 'daana in a khichdi', or a grain of rice in a pulao, but that today's youth no longer think of themselves this way. Instead, he said, 'there's a sense of "the self as a project" among millennials.' Young people today have grown up in an environment where it is second nature to learn how to document the self and present it to the world. And social media platforms are full of such examples—they're learning professional-level make up skills and showcasing them on Facebook and Instagram, they're showing off their dance skills, they're making comedy, and of course, they're documenting mundane details of their lives through barrages of selfies.

Navigating social media with their smartphones, young Indians make hundreds, if not thousands, of decisions daily: whether they are about 'liking' a photo or uploading a selfie. This new form of control is exhilarating, and the digital universe provides millennials the agency they lack in their daily lives, where they are constantly policed on their looks, interactions and behaviour. Young people constantly seek personal improvement, and define their unique identities using technology on social media. A selfie may seem trivial in comparison to Nazneen's story—but even her dramatic reshaping of her offline life began with online experiences and interactions. And in a country where patriarchy and caste system continue to influence society and the public space, social media platforms are crucial, and often the only spaces where millennials can be themselves or project versions of themselves they'd like to be.

Indian millennials harness technology to access platforms and share their views when physical spaces and societal attitudes have been designed to consign them to the background. Thirty years ago, men and women were expected to dress conservatively and not attract attention. There was no way for an aspirational young person in a small town to present herself to the outside world. Today, young India decides how it wants to present itself to the world at large. Some people like Nazneen find ways to break out of old boxes, but preserve old conventions—whether it is by promoting typical beauty standards, or espousing conventionally gym-toned bodies as ideals.

Others create and help shape more radical spaces online, such as Sumeet Samos, a Dalit rapper who harnessed the power of rap to agitate for Dalit rights, and became a millennial voice for a centuries-long struggle.

~

The Lit Boy

Sumeet Samos is an intrepid Dalit rapper from Odisha. He grew up in a *basti* in Koraput, where he rarely interacted with people from dominant castes. While getting his masters at JNU in Latin American literature, he tried joining campus politics, but found that left-wing groups were led by students from dominant castes who only wanted him to stick posters on walls.[7]

Around this time, Samos heard the legendary American rapper Tupac and found himself inspired. He started uploading his own rap videos to YouTube about his experiences of caste-discrimination, and how supposedly liberal people found it odd meeting an English-speaking Dalit.

Following Dalit scholar Rohith Vemula's suicide in 2016, Dalits across India began demanding greater justice, and Samos' videos started attracting widespread attention, regularly getting thousands of views. He launched his own YouTube channel and adopted the stage name, The Lit Boy. Since then, he has performed in campuses across India, and also in Mauritius and Paris. In a short period of time, he became one of the most prominent young Dalit voices in the country, challenging caste hegemony.

'Since I belong to a Dalit family, since childhood, I have seen how caste plays a very important role,' Samos said in a video interview.[8] 'The serious form of caste discrimination I have faced is when I scored perfectly good grades, but just because I come from a certain caste background, they [Jawaharlal Nehru University] wouldn't give me the scholarship. They wouldn't help me in getting recommendation letters. That is one of the most brutal forms of caste discrimination I have faced within JNU.'[9]

There was an edge to Samos which could have only been acquired through struggle.

Social media gave him a stage and platform to rap when most other public places weren't readily accessible to him. If it were not for YouTube, I would probably never have met Samos on 'This is Us', journalist Barkha Dutt's show, in April 2019. I was there as a panellist to talk about my research, and Sumeet had been invited to share one of his rap anthems, *Ladai seekh le* (learn how to fight). It was a metaphorical call to arms for subaltern castes and religious minorities to harness their numbers and powers and fight all systems of oppression.

In the song, Samos raps, *Maang-maang ke thak gaye, ab sab kuch lenge chheen ke* (We are tired of asking, we are now going to snatch it all).[10]

The theme of resistance runs through Samos' lyrics. He uses the internet and pop culture to articulate a call to struggle, sending a message that Dalits are a force to be reckoned with. As he says, his generation of activists is rejecting and replacing 'the framework of oppression that Dalits are always viewed through. Instead, here are people who are powerful, who have culture and art, a history, who are interesting and who can resist.'[11] For his own artistic moniker, he chose The Lit Boy, a pun on the word Dalit and the word 'lit', contemporary slang for literature.

Social media is creating a democratization of agency and access. It is providing stages and platforms to youth denied critical pathways to access opportunities. It is also bringing together communities scattered across vast physical spaces. For minorities, social media provides a meeting space to communicate when doing so in public might not be safe. For long, social and gender norms have prevented women from accessing public spaces and forums in which they can express their views and desires. Social media provides them with such a platform. It can allow victims of domestic abuse to work their way into entrepreneurial ventures and members of subaltern castes to mobilize against dominant caste oppression.

There is, of course, a downside to all of this. Many liberals in the West realized they lived in 'echo chambers' after the 2016 Brexit vote and Donald Trump's election, which alerted them to the fact that their views were not as widely shared as they had assumed. Similarly, Indian social media is also full of echo chambers—but since there are so many more fault lines in Indian society, these often become camps that are in conflict with each other. Real life caste and religious divisions find their way online, and given the relative anonymity that social media users enjoy, these divisions often become more bitter on the internet. Social media amplifies those who use it to channel outrage and negativity into the world. People are rewarded for creating attention, and they often do so by sharing controversial views or things that make them angry. In 'sharing' or 'retweeting' this content, millions more are exposed to views they may not have encountered in their local newspaper or radio show. Social media allows such information and opinion to have unprecedented reach, from cities to small towns to villages.

It has also allowed for local frictions to have effects across the country. Earlier, a tussle between neighbours or local communities remained that. Today these conflicts, especially when they have any connection to religion, become national news in mere moments. In particular, social media users are pummelled so frequently by narratives against Muslims that it becomes almost impossible for those who consume this content, even passively, to not believe some of what they see. Since 2014, the country has seen hateful boycott campaigns, numerous demonstrations of support for perpetrators of hate crimes, and the radicalizing of disaffected youth online, the effects of all of which have been multiplied because of the reach of social media.[12]

MARRIAGE AND SOCIAL VIEWS

One day in 2019, I was on the Delhi metro, on my way to an office in the Okhla industrial area. I was sitting next to a middle-aged man who looked like he was out on work as well. I was playing a game of Tetris on my phone when I happened to glance over at his screen. There was a grid of photos of young men on what looked like a dating app.

I was quite surprised. Since homosexuality is still taboo in India, I did not expect a man, particularly a middle-aged one, to peruse a dating app looking for men in the middle of the Delhi metro.

But I was seriously mistaken. He was on shaadi.com (India's number one matrimonial website), looking for young men for his daughter. I didn't talk to him, but I did keep looking at his screen, fully aware that it was rude to do so.

It appeared that he had turned some filters on, because as he clicked on their profiles, I discovered all the men on his grid were Tyagi Brahmins. If he liked someone he saw, he would send them a message that was pre-saved, which was along the lines of 'Hello, I am XYZ's father. My daughter is a light-skinned 24-year-old history graduate from Delhi.' There was more text, but it was outside my field of vision. I knew how popular matrimonial websites were but couldn't help think of the similarities between the way the man was searching for boys for his daughter on his mobile, and the way that many young men and women across the world look for partners, or even just flings, for themselves.

After getting home later that day, I logged onto the shaadi.com website to create a profile for myself. I wanted to see what it was like: what sort of questions people asked and how interactions took place. But I abandoned my plan after realizing I was uncomfortable creating a profile in bad faith. The information I was asked to enter to create a profile included details about my caste, sub-caste, gotra, skin complexion, height, educational qualifications, annual income, and diet— not very different from the information that matchmakers in India have sought for generations.

I don't know what went on at that man's house. I don't know whether he consulted his daughter or if she knew that her father spent his free moments looking for boys for her. But I do know that the old way of marriage has not changed—it has just moved online.

Over my interviews with a range of millennials across gender, caste, class and religious divides, I was struck by how often I felt like I could have been speaking to anyone from an older generation. For example, despite Bollywood movies with powerful stories about brave young couples fighting for love and chasing romance, I found that most of the country's millennials were unwilling to have romantic adventures. Arranged marriage continues to thrive across India, regardless of one's place or position in society.

One of the key tasks I set myself on when I began my fieldwork was to find out whether millennials were predominantly liberal or conservative. Two years and 900 interviews later, I discovered they were both. Millennials seek to define themselves on their own terms, even if their identities are similar to those of their parents. Every generation, one might argue, does a version of this. But millennials' new ideas of the world come straight from the West, as international media has spread rapidly through India. They have seen how the rest of the world lives in a fast-changing global landscape and crave that life, even as they seek to retain traditional values.

Therefore, marriage, because of the focus still placed on it in Indian society, is a useful lens through which one can examine millennial social views more broadly.

• ——— •

Caste in the Air We Breathe

There is north and south, east and west; there are those who speak only Hindi and those who only speak one of the myriad other regional languages; there are metropolises, Tier 1 cities, Tier 2 cities and Tier 3 cities; there are Hindus, Sikhs, Christians, Muslims, and others. Hindi-speaking and local language-fluent; urban, semi-urban, and rural; male and female; Hindu, Sikh, Christian, Muslim. And of course, there is the oldest and perhaps the most famous division of them all: the caste system.

The common perception among the professional class in urban areas that caste doesn't exist in 21st Century India is simply inaccurate. The caste system has proven to be a nimble and powerful institution, remaining a part of the air India breathes. Despite reservations and laws that prohibit caste-based discrimination, subaltern castes continue to face social exclusion, denial of opportunities at schools, colleges, and offices, and physical abuse and violence.

An extensive study published in 2015 by JNU Professor Surinder Jodhka on hiring in the corporate sector found chilling practices, particularly when it came to caste. Although hiring managers were reluctant to mention caste, they often talked about the importance of 'family background' in hiring potential employees. The HR manager of Food Futures told Jodhka and his team:

'As personal traits are developed with the kind of interaction you have with society. Where have you been brought up, the kind of environment you had in your family, home, colony, and village. These things shape up the personal attributes of people. This determines his behaviour, and working in a group with different kind of people. We have some projects abroad, and if a person doesn't behave properly with them, there is a loss for the company. Here family comes in between. Whether the person behaves well and expresses himself in a professional way, for a longer term and not for a short term. This is beneficial.'[1]

As Jodhka writes:

'Given the context, this was closely linked to their notions of caste, community and place of residence, about which they had strong opinions. In some cases, this almost directly translated into nearly complete elimination of candidates coming from reserved categories, the Scheduled Castes [SCs], Scheduled Tribes [STs] and the first-generation educated, with rural parents. Even if they were meritorious, they were unlikely to be able to speak 'good' English. Though no one admitted that they asked the candidates about their caste background, many hiring managers openly admitted their ways of 'placing' and guessing the interviewee's caste. "It is not tough to figure out their caste and social background. One gets to know about it the moment they open their mouth, the way they speak in English language", reported Mr. Jain who worked for a leading watch-manufacturing company. Several of them told us about their experience of campus hiring where they were invariably given two separate lists of candidates, first of those admitted to the course through open competition, and second of those who came in through the reserved quotas for Scheduled Castes and Scheduled Tribes.'[2]

Jodhka's career-long research on the caste-system has found that it continues to thrive in India, a conclusion seen in the work of countless other scholars.

In her book *Coming Out as Dalit*, journalist and fellow millennial Yashica Dutt documents the physical abuse, social ostracism, and denial of opportunities Dalit students face at schools, colleges, and universities:

'Ragging, institutional bullying, and lack of support for Dalit students causes many of them to commit suicide, and discourages other Dalits from applying to these important centres of learning, leading them to be excluded from these fields. This sends a clear signal to young Dalit aspirants that these prestigious colleges have no place for them, regardless of what the reservation policy dictates. The toxic belief that "quota students" are innately less able or talented than "mainstream students" is at the heart of this exclusion.'[3]

Given the historic correlation between caste and class in India, millions of young Dalit students are also at a disadvantage because of the high cost of tuition at coaching centres that prepare students for entrance examinations to elite universities. Even after admission, the path forward is not without hurdles. The lack of support structures and networks that can help them find jobs and internships makes it nearly impossible for marginalized students to succeed. As Dutt notes, in 2015, 90 per cent of the students dismissed for low grades at IIT Roorkee were SC/ST/OBC.[4] Rohith Vemula, who died of suicide in 2016 after sustained institutional harassment, is unfortunately just one example of a marginalized student who faced caste-based intimidation and violence. Almost three years after Vemula's suicide, a promising millennial doctor named Payal Tadvi hanged herself in her hostel room in Mumbai. Tadvi, a member of the Bhil Muslim Scheduled Tribe, named three of her classmates in her suicide note, accusing them of abusing her with casteist insults, and repeatedly harassing her.

In my interviews with college-educated Dalits—and to an equal extent Muslims—college always came up as a deeply uncomfortable experience. Many described truly horrific incidents of ragging and caste-based abuse. A Dalit doctor I met in Kochi, Kerala, told me how his peers at a college in Rajasthan would try and determine the category he had been admitted under. 'The first thing the boys in my hostel asked me was my NEET ranking,' he said, his voice shaking with emotion. 'They then used that to see whether I had come from the reserved quota. Since I had used reservations, they became extremely resentful and hateful towards me.'

Even though it had been more than ten years since he graduated, his emotions were raw. Holding back tears, he went on: 'They often referred to me as *bhangi*. They would tell me how

I didn't deserve my spot in the programme. They didn't know or care about how poor and uneducated my family was and how hard it was for me to make my way into a medical programme.'

It wasn't just his classmates who were resentful. Even teachers and professors routinely made lewd casteist comments, openly announcing that the bar for reserved students was lower than that for everyone else.

The data confirm this lack of support for reservations. According to the CSDS study, less than half, or 46 per cent of the youth surveyed, completely support reservations for SCs and STs in government educational institutions, and this support was very dependent on the socio-economic status of the respondent.[5] Only 28 per cent of Hindu Upper Castes and 42 per cent of Hindu OBCs 'completely support' SC-ST reservations, while 10 per cent each offer conditional support.[6] Two-thirds or 67 per cent of Hindu SCs, 'completely support' affirmative action, demonstrating a significant difference in the attitudes towards reservations, which at some level, also highlights attitudes towards caste discrimination and the measures to fix it.

Similarly, although 48 per cent of the youth surveyed 'completely support' SC-ST reservations in government jobs, attitudes break down expectedly on socio-economic status. 30 per cent of Hindu Upper Caste youth, 44 per cent of Hindu OBC youth, 71 per cent of Hindu SC youth, and 60 per cent of Hindu ST youth provide 'complete support' for these reservations, while 50 per cent of Muslim youth do the same. (Some of these responses could be attributed to social desirability bias, a phenomenon associated with field research wherein respondents occasionally give answers they think interviewers want to hear.)

~

I got a sense of how communities can often live extremely cloistered lives, rarely interacting with those from vastly different backgrounds during my appearance on Barkha Dutt's television news show, *This is Us* in April 2019. It aired on the now defunct *Tiranga TV* and was produced in a similar manner to Dutt's popular weekly show, *We The People* on NDTV. *This Is Us* had a townhall format, with a panel of speakers and an engaged audience. A day before the show—focusing on the 80 million first time voters in the 2019 general elections— one of the producers called to have me on board to share some of my research.

I was nervous and wary. Indian news debates have a well-deserved and notorious reputation for screaming, shouting and name-calling. However, *Tiranga TV* was trying to be different. Although it shut down amid a huge fracas a few months later, while it was functional, it claimed to disrupt the status quo with a focus on honest and unbiased reporting. I asked who the other panellists were going to be: peace activist Gurmehar Kaur, Aam Aadmi Party parliamentary candidate Raghav Chaddha, Youth Ki Awaaz founder Anshul Tewari, and comedian Sanjay Rajoura. I agreed to participate.

When I shared some findings from my field work, I got a very interesting reaction from the audience.

Dutt introduced me by talking about my book, and about some of my research that has found Indian millennials to be more socially conservative than previous generations—though of course, that was only a small part of my fieldwork. When I began speaking, I told her about my interview process: I asked a few standard questions, and one of them was whether my interviewees would marry outside their community. I used the term 'community' to keep it ambiguous and about nine out of every ten millennials I interviewed responded with a 'no'.

I would then follow up with another question: Would they consider marrying outside their caste or religion?

In urban areas and with respondents who were highly educated or had stable, private sector jobs, I'd often see more of an acceptance to marry outside their caste group. However, in smaller cities and towns and rural areas, most millennials told me that they would not consider inter-caste marriage. And among almost all my respondents, marrying outside their religion was totally outside the bounds of reality or imagination.

Dutt took up this point, and asked the studio audience, which was overwhelmingly young, urban, largely English-speaking, and I would assume, well-educated, whether they had relationships outside their community. In a room of about fifty people, only one hand went up.

And that was in Noida, a Delhi suburb brimming with professionals and India's upwardly mobile middle class.

One explanation for this may be the 'bubbles' many young Indians live in. A large number of well-off millennials in big cities tend to only spend time with people from a similar socio-economic background, never really interacting with individuals from 'other' communities or religions. Consider, as an example, the case of Sumeet Samos. As he tells it, many supposedly 'liberal' students at JNU were surprised to meet an English-speaking Dalit. And of course, concomitantly, socio-economic hierarchies and centuries of oppression ensured that Samos, who grew up in a basti, or ghetto, in Koraput, rarely interacted with people from dominant castes himself. This stratification was historically built to reduce mingling of different caste groups. It endures in the 21st Century.

Even in big cities, caste segregation continues to thrive. In slums in nearly every big Indian city, an unwritten social code has assigned different pockets to different caste groups. The youth in these slums, like everyone else, are extremely caste aware. Despite massive rural-urban migration in India, with millions moving to cities every year, the caste system remains largely intact, transplanted from one context to the other through intricate networks of families, friends and acquaintances.[7]

The CSDS study found 'young people to be fairly conservative on issues of marriage, live-in relationships, and dating'. It uncovered that over a third of young Indians (36 per cent) considered 'inter-caste marriage to be "completely wrong"', a quarter thought it 'partially right', and only a third 'fully approved' of it.[8] And even then, *only 4 per cent* of the youth surveyed by the CSDS team had actually had an inter-caste marriage. This was despite the fact that acceptance for inter-caste marriages had increased from 31 per cent in 2007 to 55 per cent in 2016 (including those who 'fully approved' of it and those who found it 'partially right' without by any means endorsing it).

The number is so low primarily because of the tradition of arranged marriages, which continues to thrive in the country today. Due to convenience, conditioning, and when necessary, coercion, 84 per cent of married respondents surveyed by CSDS had had an arranged marriage.[9] In contrast, only 6 per cent had had a 'love' marriage, that is, one in which they chose their own partner. And given that arranged marriages originate in family networks, they largely remain within the same caste and always within the same faith. The CSDS study found that 97 per cent of arranged marriages are between people of the same caste. This is how endogamy in the marriage market is ensured, helping keep the caste system intact.[10]

Further, from among those who had had an arranged marriage, a greater number considered the following things wrong more than right: inter-caste marriage (48 per cent said it was wrong, 43 per cent thought it acceptable), inter-religious marriage (57 per cent and 35 per cent), live-in relationship before marriage (76 per cent and 15 percent), celebrating Valentine's Day (54 per cent, and 30 per cent) and dating before marriage (66 per cent, and 25 per cent). These numbers startled me. Why would 54 per cent of respondents come out against the celebration of Valentine's Day? This question is clearly answered when you spend 14 February in small town India, where gangs of vigilantes often harass and violently attack young couples celebrating the occasion.[11] Millennials have been conditioned to accept social conservatism to preserve existing systems of power and privilege.

Inter-religious marriages were even rarer than inter-caste marriages. Only 2 per cent of the married youth surveyed had had an inter-religious marriage, while 98 per cent had a spouse from the same religion. The study found that 28 per cent approved of inter-religious marriages, 19 per cent somewhat approved, and almost half—45 percent—disapproved of them.

My interviews almost exactly mirrored the findings of the CSDS survey. Wherever I went, I would find relative acceptance of inter-caste marriage, but great reluctance towards, and more often downright opposition to marrying outside religion. But even when I would ask about inter-caste marriage, the people I met would tell me that they had no opposition to *others* having inter-caste marriages, but that they themselves had married or would marry within their caste groups.

This was most clear to me in Jaipur, where I made a last-minute dash for interviews during the Lok Sabha elections. It was the height of Indian summer, May 2019, and I spent the afternoon interviewing employees of a web services firm in the city's C-Scheme neighbourhood. The company provides a host of online services—from Search Engine Optimization (SEO) to content creation and ad placements—for businesses in India and all over the world. Its staff were not just from the city, but from all over central India. I was mainly there to ask them about how they intended to vote in the Lok Sabha showdown, but talking to them about their lives was far more interesting.

My sixth interviewee that afternoon, Riddhi Chaddha was the first Congress supporter I met in the four days that I spent in Jaipur. A self-effacing twenty-eight-year-old, Riddhi was a marketing specialist at the firm, responsible for online marketing campaigns. The moment she told me she intended to vote for 'the hand', since she was reluctant to name the Congress, I looked up from my notebook knowing that this interview would be different. But she soon followed it up by saying she wasn't interested in politics. She described herself as 'apolitical' and told me she was only voting for the Congress because that's what her family always did. She continued by telling me she *was* a Modi supporter—with an emphasis on *was*—even though she hadn't voted for him in 2014 but was disappointed by the direction in which the country, and particularly the economy, seemed to have been heading under his leadership. She knew the economy wasn't doing well; half her clients had closed their accounts at her company.

She then told me that she was going back to voting for the Congress because that's how her family had always voted, and that the relative hope that Modi had offered in 2014 had evaporated over the five years of his first term. She spoke of how her father had been a lifelong Congress loyalist. When I asked about how her husband intended to vote, she said she didn't know.

But she added that both she and her husband were 'apolitical', and that they didn't talk about politics, or for that matter, much else at home. 'We don't have many common interests,' Riddhi explained. 'When we're home, we either watch Netflix or Amazon Prime at night. We both love *FRIENDS*.'

Riddhi got married at twenty-five, to a man her aunt had suggested to her parents. She knew she would have to get married early, and after a few interactions with her prospective husband, became comfortable with him and accepted the match. Since he seemed like a nice person, and she didn't notice any red flags about him, she decided to go ahead. As is common in arranged marriages, they had almost no physical interactions before the wedding—she told me they only held hands, once. After marriage, she moved into his house, where he lived in a 'joint family' with his parents, his brother and his brother's wife.

'I didn't have any problems with him. He seemed fine when we met so I didn't object,' she said. Then, she added as an afterthought, 'Besides, my sister married outside our caste group, and she has some problems in her marriage.'

I was intrigued by this last bit of information. *What problems did her sister face?* By this time Riddhi and I had really broken the ice. She had no qualms telling me about her family, her marriage and the lives of her loved ones.

'Just,' she said, 'In her family, *unka uthna bethne ka tareekha alag hota hain.*' Although this last bit doesn't have a clear parallel in the English language, it's important to unpack it. Their way of standing up and sitting down, the most direct translation, ignores the coded nature of the message: They're different. 'They eat different from us and behave differently. This is why she sometimes has problems with her in-laws,' she said.

Before her own marriage, Riddhi had a comfortable life. She was born into an upper-middle class family, went to a convent school for her education, and got along well with her parents and her sister. They vacationed within India once or twice a year, and outside the country every two or three years. She was content with the way things were.

When the time came for marriage, she felt her parents knew best and decided to along with their plans for her life. 'My parents know me so well, and they know what's best for me,' she told me, adding with absolute certainty, 'I knew they will make the right choice.'

She told me she wanted a match from the same caste because: 'We wouldn't face any problems. It would be easy to adopt my husband's family's culture. It would have taken time for me to adapt to the rituals of another caste group.' And of course, she added, 'if we had any problems, I know my parents would support me.'

But as she began to tell me details about her own marriage, it did not seem like a particularly happy one. Like her sister, she seemed to have fairly big problems as well.

'There are many double standards,' she began. 'We both get home at around 7 p.m., but I am expected to join my sister-in-law and mother-in-law in the kitchen and cook for the men while he lays on the bed and watches television.'

'I don't mind cooking. In fact, I enjoy it. But I hate being taken for granted. Why am I always expected to wake up early or be back at home at a certain time to cook for everyone?' she asked. 'Why can't the men ever help out?'

Riddhi told me she raised this issue with her husband, who asked her 'what's your problem with helping out around the house?'

She told him she didn't have a problem, but that it was not her *duty* to serve the men at home. I was quietly listening while Riddhi asked me a bunch of questions: 'Why does the bahu have to do all of this? On Karva Chauth, why does the girl have to keep a fast? Why don't these things ever happen vice versa?'

I didn't have an answer for her, and it didn't seem like she wanted one.

She told me that, like many other women her age, she was very excited about her wedding, 'which was very modern, but our marriage is very traditional'.

'Earlier women couldn't dance in front of their in-laws,' she continued. 'Now they can. But after the wedding, everything in the marriage remains traditional.'

'After the wedding you go back into the same trauma,' Riddhi concluded.

I asked Riddhi whether things were different for her sister-in-law, her husband's brother's wife. 'Things are worse for her because the whole world is pressuring her to have a baby. It's like she serves no other purpose than produce a grandchild for this family,' Riddhi added.

I could sense the pain in her voice. She told me she shouldn't complain about her situation because her sister had it worse, but I could tell that she, in many ways, felt trapped. Her daily routine was monitored by her in-laws, her husband didn't seem particularly receptive to her concerns, and although her parents knew she wasn't happy, they felt she just needed more time to adjust to her new life.

My conversation with Riddhi left me unsettled, and I continued to think about it from time to time. A few months later, I was discussing my research and the stories I heard during my interviews with the journalist and gender specialist Namita Bhandare. A veteran writer, Bhandare had heard and seen it all. 'From the moment a young girl can think, marriage is reinforced repeatedly: in media, in film, and in daily conversation. It's the one institution that nobody is really challenging,' she said.[12]

What I had assumed to be signs of what is conventionally understood as modernity—Riddhi's job at a technology company, her Western attire, and her love for Hollywood movies and television—were just the trappings of globalism. In her own life, tradition and obedience were more important than anything else. Riddhi's life and choices are indicative of larger trends among millennials. Her marriage, arranged by her family, demonstrates how caste continues to play a dominating role in the lives of young people, unavoidably so when it comes to the marriage market. It also shows that young women in India still lack critical agency within their marriages, even if they're within their same caste networks. Riddhi, at the very least, has a stable job that pays her a good salary in case she ever needed an independent income to live on her own. But a vast majority of Indian women do not have similar financial security.

The arranged marriage system is meant to provide stability and maintain hierarchy in a country where a regimented caste system has dictated the social order for centuries. Although the institution infantilizes adults, as they are seen as incapable of making such decisions for themselves, it is justified by millions as the bride and groom are told to think beyond their own desires and instead focus on the benefit their marriage will provide to their families and overall communities. In many cases, it leads to successful unions, but it also often doesn't. Arranged marriage also puts an undue burden on women, who as the social scientist Prem Chowdhry has shown in great detail in her book, *Contentious Marriages, Eloping Couples*, are expected to protect their family and community's honour. Young women are conditioned from an early age and led to believe that they will damage the family's reputation if they choose a love marriage, and that they could lose the support of their family. Worse, they may also face physical threats to their safety and survival.

~

Dangers of Being Romeo and Juliet

One of the most interesting conversations I had in my fieldwork was at Maharaja College in Ernakulam, Kerala, considered a bastion of far-left Communist student politics. It was a hot November day, and I was there specifically to interview the young communists of the CPI(M)'s university wing, the Students' Federation of India (SFI). I had stopped at the canteen to take an evening chai break and make notes, when an affable twenty-one-year-old student named Jeff came and sat next to me.

Jeff wasn't a Communist, but a member of the Congress party's student wing in Kerala, the Kerala Students Union. He was dressed in a white shirt, blue jeans, and a silver cross hung around his neck.

He could tell I wasn't a student of Maharaja College and asked me where I was from. I answered and asked him the same question. He replied promptly, with broad walking directions to his home, which was fifteen minutes away. We then got talking and continued for more than two hours—the conversation ended only as the sun had set, and Jeff suddenly realized he needed to get home to take his grandfather to the doctor.

Jeff and I discussed a range of subjects, from culture and politics, to television and cricket. It was among the most interesting interviews I had conducted up until that point.

He began by railing about the state of politics in 'the rest of India', and insisting that Kerala was significantly different. The state had bucked the trend seen in the rest of the country in the recently concluded Lok Sabha elections in May 2019. It sent 19 Congress legislators and one Communist legislator to Parliament, despite a high-pressure BJP campaign to capitalize on the polarizing Sabarimala verdict and consolidate the Hindu vote.

'We Malayalis are different. We don't care about this Hindu-Muslim fanaticism. We treat everyone equally,' he said.

But when I asked him about marriage, he told me, 'Of course I will have an arranged marriage. My parents expect it. They will pick someone from the right background who they think is the best choice for me. I will not challenge them.'

Then, despite his pride about Kerala's liberal environment, he said, 'This is the social set-up in Kerala. They will only look for a Christian girl. They are mad about religious things like this.'

Kerala is considered India's most progressive state. It also elected the country's and the world's first Communist state government in 1957, and power has alternated between the Congress and the Communists since then. The state excels on human development indicators—all of India envies its near-universal literacy rate and relatively prosperous population. Hindus comprise nearly half of Kerala's population, followed by Muslims and Christians. It is a state where religious polarization is relatively limited compared to the rest of the country, at least on the surface, and where people go to great lengths to boast about their secular credentials. 'Every community celebrates its festivals with the other. On Onam, I go to my Hindu friends' houses, and on Christmas, they come to my house. We go to Muslim homes during their festivals and eat their food,' Jeff told me. Tightly knit religious communities live in close proximity with each other, developing intimate connections and economic interdependencies. Muslims, Christians and Hindus lend money and buy and sell products and services from each other, raising the costs of communal strife.

Bur marriage is a different matter. 'There are limitations, when it comes to marriage and relationships. They [his parents] will freak out if I find a Hindu or Muslim girl. They won't talk to me or will throw me out of the house.'

As he saw it, 'religion is very rooted in Kerala families'.

Marriage, particularly arranged marriage, is an institution that's just too big to dismantle or reform. And frankly, no one really wants to change it. As many families offer their children increasing degrees of freedom within the arranged marriage system, with more flexibility to accept or deny matches, millennials are content with the relative autonomy.

As Jeff told me, 'Since I don't want to upset my parents, I will go with whoever they choose.'

Objecting outright to getting married can be financially and physically devastating: Young people can lose shelter and their support systems and, in particularly horrific instances, in Kerala and elsewhere, become victims of honour killings.

In May 2018, the gruesome murder of Kevin Joseph, a twenty-four-year-old Dalit Christian from Kottayam, Kerala, made news across the country. In a story straight from a Bollywood film, Kevin was murdered because he fell in love with the wrong girl. The caste system hasn't spared Christianity, and Kevin's status as a Dalit Christian irked his fiancée's family, who were Latin Christians. In the early hours of 27 May 2018, two days after they had applied for a marriage registration at the sub-registrar's office in Kottayam, an armed gang arrived at Kevin's house in three vehicles, vandalizing his property, and taking him and his cousin Anish with them. They beat up Anish and left him along the way. The next day, Kevin's body was discovered floating in a nearby river.[13]

Millennials, like every other generation, are under the stranglehold of the caste-religion-marriage nexus in India.

They want greater autonomy within the system, of having the freedom to reject a match, but do not seek to reject arranged marriage altogether. In fact, more often than not, they favour arranged marriages because it takes the stress off them to find a partner.

And that's because the price of breaking out of the system—losing family contact and financial support, social exclusion and judgment from society, and physical threats to survival—is simply too high for most to challenge it. Many millennials simply cannot afford to fall in love: The risk of being cut off from their families or being evicted from their homes is too great. Given the low incomes and high cost of home ownership, many find it difficult to get by without familial support.

Even dating someone can have consequences. For years, couples in Uttar Pradesh have been terrorized by 'anti-Romeo squads', looking to find and assault young unmarried couples spending time with each other. These squads have found political patronage—largely by local leaders of religious outfits—and in the 2017 Uttar Pradesh state elections, the BJP in its manifesto even promised to create anti-Romeo squads elected to power.[14]

~

The often-contradictory responses I heard about marriage, caste and religion led me to the understanding that it's difficult to call people 'conservative' or 'liberal'. Usually, these labels are applied in the context of social issues, particularly in western debates. Conservatives typically believe in traditional values and preserving systems against disruption. Liberals largely believe in challenging the existing order to create what they consider a more just and equitable world. These definitions have different contexts in different places, and are, in many Judeo-Christian societies, particularly apparent when it comes to hot button issues such as abortion and LGBTQ rights.

Following decades of hardline policies on abortion, by 2018, overwhelmingly Catholic Ireland had legalized both abortion and same-sex marriage after consecutive referenda showed that a majority of the population had become more liberal on these two issues. The debate is very different in India, where issues such as abortion and same-sex marriage aren't among the most controversial and hotly debated ones in public discourse. Rather, it is the more explicitly religious questions that dominate, such as whether the consumption of beef should be allowed, whether India should become a Hindu rashtra, or whether minorities should have special provisions.

My research found that people can hold very hardline views on one or some of these issues, while remaining fairly unconcerned on others.

This is almost entirely due to peoples' lived experiences. Reservations, for example, is an issue which to a great extent animates individuals from dominant castes, and by extension, upper class millennials. The fact that India's education system has been left largely unimproved since Independence (apart from the setting up of a few elite institutions), and that the desire for public sector employment remains high, reservations for college seats and government jobs are a major societal flashpoint. Since the 1990s, when a student named Rajeev Goswami immolated himself to protest the implementation of the Mandal Committee's report, dominant caste anger against reservations has remained strong.

Attitudes towards reservations break down expectedly along caste lines. Those who benefit from them seek their continuation, and those from the dominant castes, who have not faced either current or historical discrimination, fight to eliminate them. Those in favour of abolishing reservations make a multi-pronged argument: They claim that reserved seats often lie vacant, that many of those admitted under quotas find it hard to keep up with the pace of academic work, and that caste-based reservations discriminate against those who may be from dominant castes, but lower class. Through my interviews, I realized that these people often find it impossible to understand the rationale behind reservations or empathize with the discrimination which many in oppressed castes continue to face in India today.

'I don't ask anyone their caste and have never seen a lower-caste person being discriminated,' a thirty-something bank manager in Pune told me. Despite the glaring contradiction in his statement, (if he didn't know his colleagues' castes, how would he know if one of them was being discriminated against on the basis of their caste?) this is a dominant view for many in the upper echelons of the caste system. But the idea at the heart of the statement, that he has never seen caste discrimination, is a further indication of how many in India continue to only interact with those from the same caste or class as them. Caste and class are closely correlated even today; as a result, people exist in large silos, shielded from interactions with those from different backgrounds.

Since people are essentially living in these compartments, they are not aware of the discrimination which exists today, even if they do not specifically hold bigoted views. Even if they consider themselves politically forward-thinking, when it comes to their personal lives, many individuals still live in the past.

~

Not *Them*

A large part of my fieldwork took place in Madhya Pradesh, and whenever I was in its capital Bhopal, I would find my way to the nearest Café Coffee Day for a reliable boost of caffeine and to get some work done. On my third visit, one of the employees asked me what kept bringing me to town, and we got talking. Originally from Odisha, Basant was a twenty-five-year-old barista. At the time we spoke, he was engaged to Rani, a girl from Kerala who had moved to Bhopal to study physiotherapy. Basant had a BBA degree from a private college in Bhubaneswar and moved to Bhopal a few months after completing his education to find a job because there was nothing available for him back home.

Though most of the young men and women I had interviewed in small towns had only met potential partners through their families, Basant had met his fiancée on Aisle, a dating application. He didn't know many people in Bhopal, so he downloaded several apps on his phone, including Tinder, Bumble and Aisle, to see what the hype was about, and perhaps meet some girls. His strategy was simple and fairly well-known among young men on these apps around the world: He swiped right on, or chose to say yes, to every girl he saw. When he matched with one, he would start chatting with her if he found her attractive. Soon, he met Rani—at the same Café Coffee Day where he worked—and they started seeing each other. Their dating began with movies at the Rang Mahal cinema and progressed to walks along the lake late at night.

Given societal taboos around sex, I was curious to know about whether they had been sexually active, but I didn't know how to ask. I beat around the bush a few times, until Basant asked me, 'would you ever buy a car without test driving it?'

I was fascinated by Basant and Rani's story. It was so incredibly different from everyone I had met before and everyone I would meet after. They belong to the 6 per cent of millennials who reported to having a self-choice or 'love' marriage. Basant's parents live in his hometown of Puri, where his mother works as a house help and his father is a building contractor. Neither had much money when they got married, as a result of which his mother was completely supportive of any decision he might take to secure a happy and comfortable life for himself. Basant and Rani were excited for the future. They were going to stay in Bhopal, where he had plans to start his own chain of cafes, and she would work as a physiotherapist.

Basant wasn't a complete outlier—some of his friends had also met their partners online, but on Facebook. Basant told me that his friends would send requests to random women they found online, in hopes of starting a conversation. The men would then send a message to anyone who accepted their friend request. According to Basant, most of his friends said that women would respond around half the time they messaged, and from there it would move forward. Two of his friends had found their partners like this. This wasn't particularly surprising—since I began my field work, I too had regularly received friend requests on Facebook from absolute strangers, sometimes just a few hours after encountering them at an event. For example, after meeting Jaiveer Shergill, a Congress politician and spokesman, I tweeted a photo with him, only to be instantly deluged with friend requests on Facebook from Congress supporters and grassroots leaders from Punjab, Shergill's home state. Some sent me messages like 'hlo sir ji', hoping to start a conversation. I prefer keeping my Facebook private, and was surprised by how many people found me and sent me messages and friend requests. My research, however, made it obvious that Facebook is used differently by most people. It is not merely a social media platform to stay in touch with friends—it is also an important tool to connect with others in ways you wouldn't have been able to earlier, allowing you to access new opportunities.

In small town India, where young people live under strict social norms, Facebook and the digital world become crucial ways for millennials to discover freedom they might otherwise lack in the physical world. Basant's friends used to sneak away in the evenings, telling their parents they were with college friends, to spend time with people they had met online. The short meetings—usually at a snack stall or an unused park—sometimes led to more substantive relationships. Two of his friends had found their partners from the same caste group so it wasn't hard convincing their parents to let them get married, but I wondered if that was a coincidence or whether they subconsciously sought out such partners.

Basant later revealed to me that Rani was from an oppressed caste. He said that it didn't really matter to him or his family. They just wanted him to marry someone who shared his values and who would look after him well. His parents had met Rani's mother, a widow and grade-four government employee, akin to a peon, at a government office in Delhi. Her father had walked out on the family when they were growing up and Rani had had to spend long hours alone as a child, while her mother worked. Listening to all of this, I decided to ask Basant if he truly would marry *anyone*. He nodded at first, but then added that while he wouldn't care about the background of most people he might date, there was one exception: He would never even think about dating a Muslim.

'Anyone but a Muslim,' he said. 'They are too different.'

I wasn't surprised. I heard this answer everywhere. Basant's more progressive views on finding a partner did not mean he had liberal views on all aspects of Indian society.

I encountered a strong prejudice against Muslims in my field research in most places I went. It is a bias that has survived generations in India, and it underlines how Indian millennials are not very different from previous generations when it comes to their social views and choices.

The ghettoization of Muslims, including in Bhopal, where they are concentrated in the old city, has led to the creation of vicious stereotypes against the community. Indian Muslims are often held responsible and answerable for perceived injustices committed by Mughal emperors and Muslim Sultans in medieval India. They are seen as outsiders and not entirely Indian by a large segment of the population and are believed by others to be Hindus who abandoned the religion. Their meat-eating habits are frowned upon by dominant castes and used as evidence to call them barbaric, while certain problematic codes in Muslim law, such as triple talaq, are used to label the community as backward. None of these biases are new; they have existed for decades, if not centuries. But barring isolated incidents of localized rioting in independent India, the Hindu-Muslim conflict has been rare at a national scale. Since 2004, however, when Atal Bihari Vajpayee's government lost the general election despite its strong performance on investment and macroeconomic indicators, certain forces in the Sangh Parivar decided to adopt a wide-ranging strategy of sustained, low-key communal violence to consolidate a Hindu vote bank. In their book, *Every Communalism: Riots in Contemporary Uttar Pradesh*, Sudha Pai and Sajjan Kumar examine a series of communal riots in Uttar Pradesh and write: 'Frequent, low-intensity communal clashes pegged on routine everyday issues and resources help establish a permanent anti-Muslim prejudice among Hindus legitimizing majoritarian rule in the eyes of an increasingly polarized, intolerant and entitled majority community of Hindus.'[15]

Although the immediate payoff is to polarize the population for electoral gain, the Sangh Parivar's longer-term goal is to move the country away from the secularism enshrined in its constitution and permanently towards a Hindu Rashtra.

This project is growing because of the increasing support from a carefully cultivated section of the population. This includes a large proportion of millennials, who were identified early on by Sangh leaders to be recruited and mobilized. As Pai and Kumar write, local Sangh affiliates are responsible for training 'a larger fuzzier group, often the educated, unemployed youth in backward states such as UP who are treated as a reservoir of support during agitations and lie dormant during lean times'.[16] The aim of these groups is to consistently keep tensions simmering between Hindus and Muslims and to let them cross the boiling point at strategic times for political advantage.

Although Basant is employed and not directly in or connected to these groups, he was exposed to their outreach on social media, particularly Facebook, where he regularly consumed pro-Modi content from his friends' feeds or pages he had liked.

It is through such propaganda that the right-wing has been fanning communal fires, leading to a spate of mob lynchings since 2014. The government has largely been silent about this hate, and in some cases, even shown support to perpetrators.

When I was back in Bhopal in August 2019, Basant was keen to discuss politics with me. The BJP government had abrogated Articles 370 and 35A of the Indian Constitution, both hotly debated provisions, which gave the state of Jammu and Kashmir relative autonomy and barred non-locals from owning land.

Basant was elated after Amit Shah's announcement, barely able to contain his happiness. I was confused. *How did this directly affect his life?*

He didn't have an answer, but he claimed that *they* had taken advantage of the state for too long. 'They took advantage of India for too long without giving anything but terrorism in return. Modi has ended that. He has shown them their place. This is the happiest day in my life.'

'They' was a code word for Muslims. And Basant had clear feelings about 'their' presence in India. 'India should be a country for Hindus, and at the time of partition they should have all gone to Pakistan.' He told me how he wanted India to, without any uncertainty, be a Hindu Rashtra.

This was an example of the Sangh Parivar's strategy paying dividends. As Pai and Kumar find, this upwardly mobile new middle class provides the most enthusiastic support for religious intolerance. This is a coalition of not just the urban rich or the growing middle class, but also better-off oppressed castes who are eager to obtain recognition and embrace a majoritarian identity after being excluded from the socio-economic mainstream for centuries.

I asked Basant if he was religious. His response was interesting: 'I am a Hindu, but I almost never go to a temple on my own. My parents rarely took me while growing up, so I went maybe once a year.'

The first part of his response was very similar to what I had heard repeatedly across the country. That many Hindu millennials, regardless of their caste, are not regular temple-goers. They are not intimately familiar with the Bhagvad Gita or other religious scripture. But they overwhelmingly identify with their religion.

The CSDS study found that India's youth were highly religious but that only a fifth, or 20 per cent of youth went to a place of worship regularly; almost double that number, or 38 per cent regularly prayed on their own.[17] Meanwhile, 48 per cent said they visited a place of worship 'sometimes', 23 per cent 'only on festivals', and 9 per cent had never been to a place of worship. Asking questions about praying, visiting places of worship, watching religious shows on television, singing devotional songs, keeping fasts, and reading a religious book, the CSDS team compiled an index of religiosity, to find that a third of youth had a low religiosity score, a quarter were moderately religious, another quarter were highly religious, and approximately one in every eight was extremely religious.[18]

None of this was surprising after I finished my first round of field interviews in February 2018, when it had become clear that being religious didn't mean visiting a temple or observing certain traditions. Religion, in most cases, was more a matter of identity than spirituality.

This is interesting, not only because of the implications it has for the future of secular democracy in India, but also because of the sharp contrasts it presents against global trends, which have found that millennials are among the least religious generations in their respective countries. Using a variety of surveys conducted between 2008 and 2017, the Pew Research Center released a report in 2018 analyzing the age gap in religion around the world. The key finding of the study was that, on several measures, young adults tended to be less religious than their elders. Across a range of countries—developing and developed—adults under the age of forty were less likely than those above forty to say that religion was 'very important' in their lives.[19] In India, Pew found there was no significant difference between older and younger generations when it came to the importance of religion in people's lives. Overall, 80 per cent of those surveyed in India said religion was important in their lives, similar to other populous nations such as Nigeria (88 per cent), Brazil (72 per cent), and Iran (78 per cent).[20]

But there's more to the story. In societies where education has become more accessible, younger generations spend more years in school and college. This is a possible reason why they tend to be less religious, since the scientific temperament inculcated by education is known to encourage individuals to question religion. What's interesting is that the opposite effect has taken place in India, as the CSDS study finds that 'a plurality of young Indians also seem to lack a scientific temper since close to half the respondents were of the opinion that religion should get precedence over science when the two clash with each other'.[21] When the CSDS team asked its respondents whether they preferred their religious beliefs to science, 47 per cent said yes.[22] Breaking that figure down, support for the proposition was the greatest among the highest educated youth—with an entire half saying they believed religion should take precedence over science, while only 39 per cent said it shouldn't. Meanwhile, among non-literate youth, only a quarter agreed that religion should take precedence over science. 14 per cent supported science, while a majority (60 per cent) had no opinion on the matter. This finding suggests that scientific temperament had not increased with an increase in education; it had, in fact, decreased. This prioritization of religion extends to other issues as well. Three out of every five youth in India supported banning movies which hurt religious sentiments.

I couldn't quite understand why millennials felt this way. Whenever I'd ask about whether something should be banned—beef, books, television shows or movies—respondents would often tell me, 'if it offends someone, we should ban it.' But they rarely ever had a response when I pointed out that anyone could be offended by anything. Some would say, if a particular act offended the majority—meaning the Hindus—it should be banned. What became clear was that the millennials I met were not overtly religious in their practices. In addition to their identity as Indians, they viewed their religion as secondary, and in some cases, as an equally important identity. Often, the Indian and Hindu identity were woven into one. This is one of the reasons why Hindutva, promoted by the BJP and its ideological affiliates, has been on the rise across India. A large and growing number of millennials agree with the idea of India as a Hindu nation. They don't necessarily believe that any non-Hindu should be treated as a second-class citizen or that Hindus should receive preferential treatment, but they have no objection if certain priorities of ideological Hindutva organizations—such as banning beef—are written into the law. One of my most memorable conversations regarding the ban on beef was at the Infosys campus in Mysore, where a thirty-something millennial asked me what was wrong with a ban on beef: 'We all are Hindus only. So why should we eat beef? And if *they* want to live here, then they should learn to live with certain restrictions so we can all be in peace.'

Just like Basant, the lady I had spoken to used the term 'they' liberally. She didn't need to explain what she meant; we both knew who she was talking about. Implicit in her statement wasn't a hatred towards Muslims, but rather a belief that it fell to them to maintain peace and live under values decided by the majority. And that's also what Basant felt: Since Muslims had chosen to remain in India, they should essentially abide by practices dictated by its Hindu majority.

~

India is defined by its diversity, and anyone seeking to make generalizations about the views of Indians must therefore tread carefully. But some generalizations are safe to make, such as in India, more than in most other countries, opportunity and success are heavily dependent on the circumstances of your birth. Caste, class, and religion continue to shape young India as much as they defined old India. It is a cycle which the country has not been able to break.

For those born into relative privilege or power, there is a great sense of reluctance when it comes to challenging the status quo. For those in the subaltern sections of society, while there is an increased appetite for radical change to better their lives, the risk and ostracization associated with fomenting this change is a high barrier to activism.

Although the world has changed tremendously in the last few decades, the stranglehold of India's caste system has not. And the data tell us that caste continues to exercise immense influence on everyday life, and in the marriage market in particular. The unchallenged popularity and prevalence of arranged marriages makes clear that parental authority has not lost ground in the country. Faced as they are with bleak economic and employment conditions, the roles of parents and extended kin may, in fact, be a larger influence in the lives of millennials than any other generations.

Riddhi and Basant are young, aspirational, middle-class Indians.

Riddhi is someone who is well established in middle-class India. Both she and her husband have well-paying jobs in a city where the cost of living is fairly affordable. She expects to have a baby soon and will quit work to take care of her child. In more ways than one, she embodies the new Indian middle class: aspiring, upwardly mobile, yet traditional. As Riddhi is questioning existing systems of power and privilege, she also feels trapped by those very systems. Despite her challenges, she told me she would continue doing what was expected of her as she'd rather live a comfortable, predictable life than risk what she had. Either through conditioning or coercion, millions of millennials have similar stories.

However, Riddhi also falls into the minority of millennials I met while researching this book: She was a Congress voter. Her political choice, although not deeply articulated, suggested a willingness to see beyond the narrative the government had been peddling prior to the election.

Basant had a love marriage. He met his fiancée on a dating app. He worked his way into India's middle class; he wasn't born into it. His family didn't care about his wife's caste, and they seemed to have a very happy relationship. The couple went out for movies together and made trips to nearby heritage sites. They seemed more compatible than Riddhi and her husband. But though in some ways, Basant was progressive and liberal, in others he was rigid and traditional. He vehemently disagreed with many of India's founders, who sought to build a secular democracy with equal rights for everyone. He wanted the country to be steeped in the Hindu ethos.

When I began my conversations with them, I expected Riddhi's and Basant's stories to end differently. I couldn't quite square one aspect of their views and personalities with the other.

This was the most fascinating contradiction in my research. It showed me that there was truth behind the cliché that any truism about India could immediately be countered by another truism about India. For example, for every Fortune 500 CEO produced by an IIT or IIM, there are millions of unemployable graduates produced by public or private colleges, unskilled for a global economy hurtling towards automation. Similarly, even though the country is home to millions in extreme poverty, it has the world's third largest number of billionaires, and is roughly estimated to add three billionaires every month.[23] But the truest version of this truism about truisms is captured in a truth about Indian millennials: for every young Indian who challenges society, there are ten who spend their lives conforming to it.

POLITICAL ATTITUDES

Ever since the 1996 general elections, when PV Narasimha Rao's government lost its majority after embarking on India's economic liberalization, and the 2004 general elections, when Atal Behari Vajpayee lost power despite India's top-line macroeconomic successes, political parties have doubled down on their strategies of social engineering to win power. The 2004 Congress campaign was unabashedly pro-poor and pro-farmer, helping the party snatch an unexpected victory from an incumbent that ran on a slogan of 'India Shining', which may have seemed true in corporate boardrooms, but rang hollow on the ground. The first Congress-led UPA government, in alliance with Communist parties, implemented the National Rural Employment Guarantee Act, one of the world's largest labour guarantee programs, passed the Right to Information Act, signed a landmark civil nuclear deal with the United States, and presided over a fast-growing economy.

In the 2004 and 2009 elections, there was no distinguishable pattern to how young voters cast their ballots—their political behaviour was similar to that of older age groups. But things began to change soon.

The second UPA tenure was almost the opposite of the first. Legislative lethargy, multiple corruption scandals, an acute agrarian crisis, and a series of terrorist attacks laid the ground for political change and disruption. Voters were fed up of the government, which seemed more interested in lining its own pockets than creating prosperity for citizens.

The country had also transformed since the new millennium. A big demographic shift had made India much younger. After decades of penury, there was now a rapidly growing middle class living in an increasingly urbanizing country with greater exposure to the media than ever before. Many continued to live in harsh poverty, but this new middle class had a growing influence on the political narrative and the children of this new class were more aspirational than their parents.

This was the time when millennials were coming of age. As they began to access the internet, finish college, enter the workforce, and start their families, they saw a country that was in chaos and an economy that was slowing down. In the run up to the 2014 general elections, it appeared that only one man had a plan to put an end to this instability and fix India. That man was Narendra Modi.

In the 2009 election, turnout among millennial voters (aged 18–25) was 54 per cent, four percentage points lower than the national average. In 2014, it swung up to 68 per cent, two percentage points higher than the national average. Not only were these young voters the most active segment of the electorate, but they were also the most pro-BJP in their voting. The party's share of young voters was 34.4 per cent, more than three points higher than its average vote share of 31.1 per cent.[1] From the 2014 and 2019 elections, a clear pattern had emerged: Young and millennial voters had become the most enthusiastic supporters of the BJP, and particularly, of Narendra Modi.[2]

Ahead of his first win, the media saturated the public sphere with round-the-clock adulation of Modi as he promoted his vision of an India with world-class infrastructure, top quality jobs, and a renewed standing on the global arena. It also helped that he projected himself as a son of the soil—an Indian success story, a leader who only had the national interest at heart. His story was that of someone who had risen from the lowest sections of society to lead his home state of Gujarat towards prosperity, and now he promised that to the rest of the country. But this was only one aspect of his appeal. Both explicitly and implicitly he held out a vision of an India where Hindus and Hindu values would be prioritized. And in the years since his win, the country's ideological median has shifted steadily to the right, so that such sectarian views are no longer confined to the fringes.

To be sure, the political attitudes of millennials are not limited to merely support for one prime minister or one political party. Rather, they are shaped by beliefs, aspirations, and anxieties that one party has been early to recognize. These impulses will be key to the future of the country, as millennials grow older and increasingly occupy positions of economic and political power.

A Wave of Change

The 2014 general elections were the first in India in which the millennial voter played a major, and in many ways, decisive role. This was when the Modi-led BJP, swept to power.

In the run up to the elections, there were clear signs that the United Progressive Alliance (UPA) government was on a weak footing. Manmohan Singh was in his second term as prime minister, and although he was lauded for being a sharp technocrat, there was little to suggest that he understood the pulse of the country's growing population. A measured and soft-spoken individual, Singh had never won a direct election and was brought into Parliament through the Rajya Sabha. He did not have his own, distinct, political constituency and was widely viewed as a proxy of then Congress president Sonia Gandhi. The National Advisory Council often described his as a shadow Prime Minister's Office.

Going into the elections, the economy was not doing well. Given India's heavy reliance on imported oil, the sharp increase in the price of crude was draining the government of precious foreign exchange and leading to high levels of inflation. Sluggish job growth and a series of high-profile cases of gruesome rapes and crimes against women gave the opposition a narrative with which to attack the government and say that it was weak on the economy and even weaker on security. But the nail in the coffin for Singh's government was the widespread resentment that had been fomenting against the bureaucratic and political corruption his administration was believed to be steeped in.

It was in this environment that Modi, then the chief minister of Gujarat, launched his campaign as the BJP's prime ministerial candidate. He touted the 'Gujarat model of development', describing the state as an investment haven with the best roads, high rates of growth, and widespread economic prosperity, all of which drew foreign companies to its shores to manufacture goods. Modi criss-crossed the country, outlining a similarly positive vision for India. His messaging struck a chord with young voters, middle class voters, agricultural voters, women voters, and voters who were simply fed up with the incumbent government. He promised to create millions of jobs every year, electrify villages, build world-class bullet

trains, and protect Indians from foreign and domestic enemies.
Capitalizing on local anxieties, Modi, in fact, asked voters not
to elect him as India's next prime minister, but as the nation's
chowkidar, or security guard. In a fiery speech in October 2013
in Jhansi, he told the audience that if they did elect him as their
chowkidar, he would go and sit in Delhi, and stop its elite from
stealing from the nation's coffers.[3]

The audience, mostly younger and male, loved it, and Modi
doubled down on this message as the campaign progressed.[4]
The electorate was tired of the litany of scandals surrounding
UPA II. The approximately 150 million millennials newly
added to the country's voting rolls could not relate to the
Congress' leadership or its confusing platform, which did not
focus on any issue in particular, but rather on a food-security
bill it had passed.[5] The legislation, also known as the 'Right
to Food Act', was passed in 2013 and was viewed by Congress
insiders and loyalists as a silver bullet that could possibly save
the party from a total washout in the 2014 elections.

But it did not work because the fundamental calculation
behind the law, that Indians wanted food security, was based on
a misreading of the electorate. Yes, they wanted food security,
but the millions of India's newly minted middle class wanted
more than just the bare necessities. These people wanted good
jobs for themselves and their children, they wanted better roads
and infrastructure—they wanted to thrive, not survive. India
had transformed from a country defined by its needs to one
defined by its aspirations. This new country was frustrated with
the lack of jobs, the slow pace of development, the constant
corruption, and the out-of-control inflation.

Modi's pitch to these voters focused on his Gujarat model
of development. He told them that in Gujarat he had been
able to create a hospitable investment climate which laid the

foundation for a new middle class and created thousands of meaningful manufacturing jobs for its youth. He understood that most of these aspirational voters had broken out of poverty. They no longer needed the essentials that the Congress was offering them. They now wanted opportunity. The other side of his record in Gujarat—having presided over the 2002 Godhra riots when nearly 800 Muslims were killed in retaliation for the murder of 58 Hindu pilgrims returning from Ayodhya—was an asset, not a liability, to his pitch. Not only would Modi create jobs and prosperity, but he would also guard the interests of the Hindu majority.

Perhaps more importantly, Modi identified that the Gandhian idea that India lives in its villages no longer held true. Millions of Indians were relocating to the country's ever-growing metropolises, and millions more were in smaller towns and cities that were rapidly expanding. Modi recognized that there was tremendous uncounted urbanization taking place in India. This 'messy' or 'hidden' urbanization was the subject of a 2015 World Bank report that pegged India's urbanization at 55 per cent, almost double the 31 per cent figure released in the 2011 Census.[6] The urban/rural divide was no longer as clear as it was at the dawn of the new millennium. The new electorate lived differently, and therefore had an entirely different set of ambitions and concerns.

Modi understood that the millions of first-time voters on the electoral rolls did not have strong ideological or partisan attachments. They had seen ten years of Congress rule, and like the rest of the country, were ready for change. So, he gave millennials a vision they could be proud of—of a strong India with millions of jobs for its youth, bullet trains from city to city, and a new middle class. Who wouldn't want to sign up for such an offer?

These aspirational millennial voters were not excited by technocratic economists nor would they be won over by basic welfare measures such as food protection laws. They wanted a new India and Modi was the only person who was promising it. The Congress was in hiding, without a core message, or a prime ministerial candidate with grassroots appeal. Modi was the only politician in the arena who understood these desires of the electorate.

Modi repeatedly reminded voters of his origins as a server of tea at his father's stall. He propagated the narrative that he did not rise to become the chief minister of Gujarat because of the family he was born into, but because of hard work and public service. He was a perfect contrast to his chief opponent: the Congress's fifth-generation dynast, Rahul Gandhi. Modi didn't just talk about aspiration—he wore it. In discarding the politician's traditional garb of a white kurta and pajama for stylish kurtas of many colours, he projected himself as a cutting-edge, new-age politician.

The 2014 elections will be remembered as the first Indian elections when social media and technology were central to party campaigns. In the 2008 and 2012 US Presidential elections, Barack Obama built tremendous support among millennial voters not only because of his policies and his message, but also through careful social media targeting and voter profiling.[7] The BJP used a similar strategy in 2014, blanketing television screens, social media networks, and newspaper front pages with flashy advertisements featuring Modi front-and-centre. Its advertising budget alone was estimated to be around Rs 5000 crore.[8] Given its money power, it successfully turned the elections into an American-style presidential contest, portraying Modi as a strong leader against a corrupt and divided opposition. In an empirical analysis of the role first-time voters played in the

2014 elections, political scientists Deepankar Basu and Kartik Misra, wrote, 'In a significant departure from the past, the BJP evoked the imagery of a masculine and decisive leader which found great resonance with the highly hierarchical nature of Indian society.'[9]

In May 2014, Modi vaulted into the Prime Minister's Office, after leading the BJP to a victory in which it captured more seats in Parliament than it ever had before. The party won 282 out of the total 543 seats on its own, enough to form the government without the support of any allies. The BJP and its pre-poll partners in the National Democratic Alliance together won 336 seats. After the election, the map of India was painted saffron all the way from Kashmir down to Goa, and from the coastal communities of Gujarat to the hills of Assam. The BJP was unsuccessful in states with regionalist parties, such as Tamil Nadu, Odisha and West Bengal, and fared poorly in the Communist bastion of Kerala. But even in these states it substantially increased its vote share—more than doubling it, for instance, in Bengal.[10] The BJP swept, or nearly swept many states, including Rajasthan, Gujarat, Madhya Pradesh and Chhattisgarh. In Uttar Pradesh, home to the Gandhi dynasty, voters handed the party 71 of the state's 80 seats. The only two seats won by the Congress were those that belonged to Sonia Gandhi and Rahul Gandhi. Established heavyweights were felled by relative newcomers and in a stunning upset, the Bahujan Samaj Party, the political home of the state and the country's Dalits, failed to win even a single seat.

A political reordering had occurred in Uttar Pradesh and most of Hindi-speaking India. Traditional caste dynamics and economic ties were broken by the Modi wave. He reduced the Congress to such a humiliating defeat, limiting it to just 44 seats out of more than 500, that the party did not even meet the 10 per cent threshold needed for it to claim the Leader of the Opposition position in Parliament. Amit Shah and Modi's dream of a 'Congress-mukt Bharat' looked like it could soon become a reality. Subsequently, the BJP consolidated its power by winning several state elections, in Maharashtra, Jharkhand, Assam, and the all-important Uttar Pradesh. It even toppled the two-and-a-half-decade-old Communist government from its bastion in Tripura. Young voters played a key role in turning all these states saffron. Regionalist parties, capitalizing on local cleavages and insecurity around the imposition of Hindi as a national language, had done well, but regional parties that appealed to certain vote banks in specific areas of the country had been annihilated.

At the time of the 2011 Indian Census, there were 120 million people aged between fifteen and eighteen. These millennials were too young to vote in 2009 and became first time voters in the 2014 elections.[11] They formed 10 per cent of the country's total population and approximately 15 per cent of the eligible electorate.

In Obama's signature words, these voters were 'fired up'. Just as Obama used his base of young voters to win the keys to the Oval Office twice, Modi wooed his new young admirers, and persuaded them to turn up and vote to support him. And the data proved it, most prominent of which was the Lokniti elections project at the CSDS, which used Census and post-poll surveys to estimate turnout among young voters in elections from 1999 onwards. Their findings revealed that in the 2014 general elections, turnout among young voters (aged 18 to 25) was 68 per cent, two percentage points *higher* than the all-India turnout.[12] This is particularly important because in previous elections, youth turnout had been substantially lower than all-India turnout. In the 2009 elections, for instance, 54 per cent of young voters cast their ballots, compared to 58 per cent of the total electorate, and in 2004, the gap was even wider, at six percentage points. On average, the turnout of young voters has generally been five to six percentage points lower than that of the national electorate. That changed in 2014.

This is important because the same Lokniti analysis highlights that these young voters decisively broke in favour of one party: the BJP. 'The vote share of the BJP amongst young voters was 34.4 per cent, more than three percentage points higher than its average vote share of 31.1 per cent,' wrote Professor Sanjay Kumar at CSDS. These young voters, aged 18 to 25, were all millennials.

Given the sheer number of young voters, even these small percentages make a huge difference, and demonstrate a clear preference for the BJP. According to data released by India's Election Commission, there were, on average, roughly 90,000 first-time voters in every constituency in 2014, making them a crucial bloc. At the time, P Muralidhar Rao, the BJP General Secretary responsible for its youth wing, the Yuva Morcha, revealed that 'the psychology of the young voter is unpolluted. These voters are bound to be more agitated about corruption, price rise and the lack of job opportunities. For them, good governance will be the issue.'[13] The data confirmed this. The CSDS study revealed that only around half of Indian youth identified themselves with any party. This lack of political identification should not be viewed as disillusionment with politics or political apathy—rather, these voters should be seen as non-partisan swing voters.

Even if these young voters had joined their families in voting for the BJP, the fact that they were turning out in such large numbers was key to the success of Modi and his campaign. Because India's first-past-the-post system hands victory to the candidate who wins a plurality of votes—which doesn't necessarily mean they have won a majority—turnout becomes increasingly important in such elections. Without a base of highly enthusiastic voters, the party could have seen a very different election result.

Basu and Misra's empirical analysis of the BJP's 'demographic dividend' is particularly revealing.[14] Using a cross-state regression model, after controlling for the percentage of rural people; state domestic output; the proportion of Muslims, SCs and STs; literacy levels; and the effects of urbanization, prosperity, religion, caste and literacy, they found that on average, if the number of first-time voters in a state had gone up by one percentage point from 2009, the BJP gained a 3.7 percentage point increase in vote share compared to the previous elections. Therefore, it is no coincidence that the BJP performed best in states that had particularly large proportions of 18–22-year-olds who had never voted before. In fact, CSDS found that the BJP had exactly twice the support of first-time voters than the Congress party, indicating clear support for the saffron party among young people.

~

Bold Action

Analyzing how millennials react to policy decisions makes one thing clear: They favour quick, bold action, no matter its consequences. This is evident from their attitudes towards Prime Minister Modi's announcement on 8 November 2016, a historical day for many reasons. Many in the West will remember it fondly, or with horror, as the day voters in the United States elected businessman Donald Trump president.

In India, 8 November is remembered for different reasons. At 8.15 p.m., when most Indians were eating dinner, Prime Minister Modi addressed the nation in an unscheduled televised address.

'There comes a time in the history of a country's development when a need is felt for a strong and decisive step,' he began. 'For years, this country has felt that corruption, black money and terrorism are festering sores, holding us back in the race towards development.'[15] He then went on to announce that in less than four hours, at midnight, most of the physical currency people held would no longer be accepted as legal tender. In a move called 'demonetization,', 86 per cent of the total currency in circulation, would become invalid. Indians would have to exchange their old notes for new ones. 'The Rs 500 and Rs 1000 notes hoarded by anti-national and anti-social elements will become just worthless pieces of paper. The rights and the interests of honest, hard-working people will be fully protected,' Modi continued in his address.

The chaos that a move as secretive and unprecedented as demonetization unleashed was immediately apparent. The next day, people formed hours-long queues outside government banks to trade old notes for new ones. ATMs hadn't been reconfigured to the dimensions of the new notes, resulting in malfunctions and a breakdown in the supply of currency. Real estate sales fell off a cliff, causing a massive disruption in India's construction industry, one of the biggest providers of employment in the country. Almost all commercial activity was halted or severely disrupted. Most tragically, the stress inflicted by the decision led to a spate of deaths across the country, including by suicide, and by exhaustion and cardiac complications while waiting in interminable queues. The government quickly began making amendments to the policy, exempting certain businesses from penalties, and shifting its explanations for the rationale behind the move.[16] For the next month or so, newspaper front pages almost exclusively carried images of the hundreds of millions impacted by demonetization—those in the long queues outside ATMs, traders lamenting about the sharp decline in commerce, and business owners with empty storefronts. It soon became clear that while it may have been well-intentioned, it was not well-planned.

Sadanand Dhume, a Resident Fellow at the American Enterprise Institute, and a self-described 'disappointed' supporter of the prime minister, wrote a strongly worded op-ed in the *Wall Street Journal* calling demonetization a 'debacle', stating that its most 'significant casualty may well be Prime Minister Narendra Modi's reputation as a sound economic manager.'[17] He also described it as a policy that would have been considered radical for even a country like Venezuela.[18] The condemnation of demonetization from economists and analysts was so widespread that even *Forbes* magazine's Editor-in-Chief Steve Forbes took to the opinion pages, labelling it 'sickening and immoral'.[19]

Indian millennials view demonetization differently.

Most of the people I interviewed for this book saw it as a bold decision to root out endemic corruption and 'black money' from Indian society. They saw it as the kind of disruptive measure that only someone who, in their view, as 'courageous' as Modi, could undertake. Whenever I interviewed millennials about politics, I would ask them to list two to three policies of the leader they were supporting. Among Modi-supporting millennials, demonetization was mentioned almost nine out of ten times. I remember in particular, one respondent who was a member of the new hire programme at Infosys in Mysore, telling me how he had goosebumps when the prime minister announced the policy. He then went on to tell me how he believed it was a systematic effort to extend formalized banking to millions of Indians, who would now get access to modern bank accounts after being forced to deposit their old notes. However, a study conducted by IFMR LEAD found that demonetization had a negligible impact, or no impact at all, on savings, banking and digital finance.[20] Nevertheless, even among those who do not support Modi, demonetization is often cited as an example of a wise decision, something more politicians should adopt as tough measures to fight corruption and solve the country's problems.

While Amartya Sen's description of demonetization as a 'despotic act' was meant to criticize the policy, many millennials supported the move precisely because it was forced on the people with no consultation.[21] One of the most common responses I heard in my interviews of those who supported the policy was that 'no one else would have done it'. Many of these individuals told me that demonetization affected them to a certain extent. One respondent, a highly educated computer engineer whose father-in-law was admitted in hospital at the time, found it almost impossible to get the money to pay for his procedure and had to frantically run around town trying to find new currency. But she, like many other supporters of the move, nevertheless said she 'loved' demonetization since it was a 'bold move'.

Modi, the master politician, knew that he won the election in 2014 in large part because the country was fed up with the scandals of the UPA-II government. Addressing his critics in remarks made almost a week after announcing demonetization, a teary-eyed prime minister made an appeal to the country in stark *us* versus *them* terms: 'They thought if they pull my hair, I will stop and do nothing. I will not be cowed down. I will not stop doing these things, even if you burn me alive.'[22] He went on: 'My dear countrymen, I gave up everything ... my home, my family. I gave up everything I had for this country.'

Those expecting an economic argument for demonetization were left disappointed. Many wanted to know how, despite all the hardship, the country's economy would, in fact, rebound and benefit from the move. But what the country got instead was a deeply emotional plea designed to get shared on social media—and of course, emotional arguments are much more persuasive than complex technocratic jargon in eliciting support and sympathy.

Listening to young Indians talk about their support for demonetization made something clear to me: This is a generation that supports bold action. That millennials may have personally been affected, positively or negatively, by such bold moves is immaterial. The fact that someone has the courage and the conviction to carry out such an action is what's important to this generation.

~

This support for bold actions translates to almost every other political and policy decision as well. In another popular move, about a month before demonetization, the Modi government launched 'surgical strikes' against Pakistan in retaliation for an attack on an Indian military camp in Uri, a small town in Jammu and Kashmir in September 2016. India has a long history of cross-border attacks perpetrated by terrorists trained in Pakistan, many of whom have been trained and supported by elements within the Pakistani Army, which uses them to pursue its strategic aims against India. The most scarring attack took place on 26 November 2008, when terrorists from Pakistan arrived in Mumbai in a boat to kill innocent civilians at high profile locations around the city and lay siege to the Trident-Oberoi Hotel complex and the iconic Taj Mahal Palace Hotel in Colaba. Although there was unanimous consensus among global intelligence agencies that the Pakistani state had backed the attackers, the Congress government did not respond with military measures. After the 2008 attacks, the Congress came back to power against a haphazard opposition, and different events captured the news cycle, but one attitude began to take root: the desire for a strong, muscular India. Indians, particularly young Indians who were coming of age, did not want to live in what they considered a 'weak country' anymore. This new India would need to fight fire with fire.

The Uri attack, which occurred two years after Modi's election, brought back traumatic memories of 26/11. Terrorists infiltrated the border in September 2016 and ambushed an Indian Army brigade camped in Uri, killing 19 soldiers. But this time something had changed: It became clear that the Indian government would have to respond. Behind-the-scene consultations and talks with foreign governments would no longer suffice as a response.

So, less than two weeks after the Uri attacks, the Indian Army announced that in the middle of the night of 29 September, it had conducted 'surgical strikes' across the border in Pakistan, airdropping special operation commandos to kill terrorists and destroy supporting infrastructure. While exact figures are unclear, it was claimed that between thirty-five and fifty terrorists were killed in those four hours.

The reaction in India was nothing short of jubilant. 'I am so happy, they should have done this much earlier,' a young woman in Mumbai told the India TV television channel. 'This was the perfect response,' she continued.[23] 'This is just the beginning for Pakistan. We are going to kill them,' another young woman in her group added.

The attacks had become so popular that the bitterly divided political system was forced to come together to congratulate the prime minister. Sonia Gandhi, the then president of the Congress, called it a 'strong message that [conveyed] our country's resolve to prevent further infiltration and attacks on our security forces and our people,'[24] while Arvind Kejriwal, Delhi Chief Minister and frequent Modi antagonist, saluted the Army, tweeting 'Bharat Mata Ki Jai. The entire country is with the Indian Army'.[25] From its official account, the BJP tweeted that the strikes signalled 'the rise of a new India'.

News of the surgical strikes spread like wildfire in India, covered extensively by television and print news, and magnified by social media and WhatsApp. The undertone to the reporting and narrative was that India had finally asserted itself, that Modi was responsible for its new strength. In such an environment, asking for more information or scrutinizing the details of the strikes would have been political suicide.

So I never found it surprising that the surgical strikes were the second most popular policy mentioned in my interviews. Even among millennials who did not support the BJP or Modi, the surgical strikes were brought up as something everyone in the country should be proud of. They gave young people the sense that the new India under Prime Minister Modi was a force to be reckoned with. While a vast majority of the young Indians I interviewed did not know intricate details about the attacks—such as the number of terrorists supposedly killed— they all praised them as a necessary retaliation to avenge the loss of Indian lives.

The surgical strikes continued to be thrust back into the public domain. On their two-year anniversary in 2018, the government organized a series of events across the country to commemorate and celebrate the occasion. Dubbing it 'Surgical Strike Day', the prime minister inaugurated an exhibition in Jodhpur called *Parakram Parv*, which flaunted the prowess of the Indian military. In Delhi, the government reportedly spent Rs 80 lakh, or more than $100,000, to pay Kailash Kher and Sukhwinder Singh, two prominent Punjabi singers, to perform at a celebration on the grounds of the India Gate in honour of the strikes.[26] Through these events, Modi and the BJP sought to take control of the news cycle and redirect public attention to the strikes.

The surgical strikes even received the silver screen treatment. In January 2019, a Bollywood film called *Uri: The Surgical Strike* was released with the up-and-coming actor Vicky Kaushal playing Major Vihaan Shergill, a strapping Army officer who not only creates strategy but also engages in hand-to-hand combat with terrorists and outsmarts seasoned intelligence operatives. The film set the cash registers ringing, becoming one of the highest earning Bollywood movies in 2019. Key to its popularity was its message: India could take the fight to its enemies and would no longer sit back or pull its punches when hit. It gave the masses a group of valiant heroes led by a confident, intelligent and brawny commando to cheer. After Shergill and his men avenge India's losses, the film ends with the soldier enjoying a formal dinner with Pallavi Sharma, an undercover intelligence agent, and India's prime minister.

I happened to be in Jaipur a week after the film released. The line for entry to the afternoon screening stretched out onto the road, with many there to see the film for their second or third time.

~

The smartphone and internet boom in India has led to an unprecedented proliferation of information. Practically anyone with a smartphone can access the news minutes after it has broken. Facebook and WhatsApp, more than social networks, are news channels. To discuss the role of social media in shaping political opinions, I met Shivam Shankar Singh, a political strategist and data analyst who worked for the BJP to help it snatch political dominance in India's northeast, where the party previously had no presence. Minutes into our conversation, I realized that Singh, a fellow millennial, was a seasoned political operative.

'There's an aspect of virality to everything,' Singh said to me, summarizing the BJP's sophisticated social media operation in one sentence. By focusing on creating content designed to go viral, the party seeks to dominate the narrative before anyone else can. To achieve this, the BJP and its allies have carefully built an echo chamber to circulate their talking points, shape the narrative, and denigrate its opponents. It does this through a host of WhatsApp groups and allied Facebook pages with names such as 'Nation with NaMo' or 'The Indian Eye'. These pages, which have millions of followers, are filled with pro-BJP memes, photos and videos, designed to be aggressive and shareable. They break down complex issues into simple false binaries, making it seem that if you don't support the prime minister, you are 'anti-national'. In this world, it's black or white. Whether its demonetization or the reaction to the February 2019 Pulwama terror attack, in which forty Indian security personnel were killed by a suicide bomber targeting their bus, you're either with the government, or against the nation. These messages are amplified through followers and expensive advertising campaigns. An analysis by the factchecking portal *AltNews* found that in the period between 7 February and 2 March 2019, 70 per cent of political advertisements on Facebook were bought by BJP or pro-BJP pages.[27] One pro-BJP page *Bharat ki Mann ki Baat* alone spent more than Rs 1.2 crore on advertisements and promotions.

I wrote this section shortly after the horrific Pulwama bombing, and the reaction to the attack, when the subsequent calls for revenge were revealing. In one *Game of Thrones* style meme, a steely-eyed Modi with the silhouettes of black-ops commandos behind him, loudly calls for war. White text in all capitals loudly declared, 'AFTER PULWAMA ATTACK, WE HAVE NOW GIVEN OUR ARMED FORCES A FREE HAND TO ACT AGAINST TERROR - PM MODI. THE GAME BEGINS NOW'. Modi had said these words at a political rally earlier in the day, and they became meme content shortly after.

At another rally in Jhansi on the same day, Modi drew up a stark contrast with the previous government. 'Our neighbouring country has forgotten this is an India of new policies and new customs,' he proclaimed.[28] With its Hindutva roots and message of cultural nationalism, national security is the most obvious arena in which the BJP can draw a stark contrast with the opposition. Key to Modi's image and approval among young voters is his determination to keep Indians safe. While this is a pitch made to all Indians, regardless of age, millennials are one of the most concerned groups about terrorism and safety, according to data. It ranked as the third most important concern for millennials, right after corruption and unemployment, a 2017 Hindustan Times Youth Survey showed.[29] Although I generally view such surveys with scepticism, particularly the ones conducted online, as well as in my own field interviews, I found that national security and India's image as a strong, powerful nation, were top priorities among millennials.

The Modi government retaliated against Pakistan thirteen days after Pulwama, launching air strikes on a terrorist camp in Balakot, deep inside Pakistani territory. It was the first time Indian jets had ventured into and hit targets in Pakistan since the 1971 war, which led to the creation of Bangladesh. In terms of pure politics, the Balakot airstrikes were gold. In avenging India's martyrs at Pulwama, Modi was able to tap into the nation's deep militaristic instincts, particularly among its millennials, to create a rally 'round the flag effect'.

Social media was jubilant. #IndiaStrikesBack and #JaiHind were trending on Twitter and Facebook shortly after 9 a.m., when most of the country started receiving news of the air strikes. Even the most liberal and anti-war Indians declared some measure of approval for the retaliation. The thinking went that Pakistan needed to be taught a lesson, and that the air strikes were proof that India could strike targets deep in its hinterland.

The media has played a key role in creating and nurturing these sentiments. Millennials grew up in the post-Kargil media environment. During Kargil, the country's first televised war, Indians saw and heard continuous, instant updates about the loss of their soldiers in the high hills of Kargil at the hands of Pakistanis. They saw the bodies of slain soldiers coming back to grieving families for their last rites. This wasn't information to be memorized from a textbook—it played out in front of them.

The Kargil war was soon followed by numerous high-profile terrorist attacks, including an ambush on India's Parliament in 2001, serial bombings in Delhi in 2005, train bombings in Mumbai in 2006, and the 26/11 attacks in Mumbai in 2008. Given the role of terrorism in Pakistan's strategy against India and its hand in these attacks, Indian public had become tired of Pakistani predation. Millennials came of age in this violent decade. They were fed up with Pakistan consistently attacking India through terrorist proxies and were unable to understand the restraint displayed by the Manmohan Singh government. Thus, it is not entirely surprising that this post-Kargil generation is more hawkish than other generations. The November 2008 attacks took place when older millennials were turning twenty-five and younger millennials were in their early teenage years. As Carnegie scholar Ashley Tellis writes, 'India has been a perpetual prisoner of its own self-restraint, so the fact that is has now changed the playbook is the story. I think Indians are now simply tired of being the punching bag for Pakistani terrorism.'[30]

On the one hand, Indians had grown increasingly agitated by Pakistani terrorism. On the other, internet and social media boom meant that information was accessible to everyone—although it became less reliable and prone to partisanship. Politicians no longer needed newspapers or television channels to broadcast their messages. They could do so directly on social media, allowing them to capitalize on existing insecurities and build their own narratives. In ostensibly putting Pakistan in its place, not only did Modi and his party defend India, but they also capitalized on the insecurities many Hindus have had about Muslims, who, according to them, had long been allowed to get away under minority-appeasing Congress governments.[31]

~

Digital Natives

With the proliferation of smartphones, and the accompanying adoption of social media, political leaders have the perfect opportunity to target their messaging. In India, like in many other parts of the world, right-wing politicians and entities have established a stronghold on this new terrain.

Although data on Facebook usage are hard to obtain and English-language pages form a fraction of the pro-Modi content on social media, there is a clear 'divide and rule' undertone to polarize the generation along religious lines. Subscribers to these pages are fed hyper-nationalist messaging against India's opponents. What is interesting about the Indian context is that it does not focus on policy, but on personality. The classic liberal versus conservative or even left-wing versus right-wing debates do not play out in this fight. Modi is constantly propped up as a strongman leader who takes bold, decisive action against enemies both foreign and domestic, as opposed to Rahul Gandhi, whom the BJP has nicknamed Pappu, or an unserious country bumpkin. According to the BJP narrative, Gandhi is a gaffe-prone, man-child dynast, who can never understand or feel the pulse of the real India the way the chaiwala prime minister can. This image has been so aggressively promoted in the BJP's social media ecosystem that it is almost accepted as a truth and often finds mention in traditional media. In my conversations with millennials, regardless of their geographical locations, socio-economic status, or levels of education, I found it striking how many people mentioned they couldn't vote for the Congress because of Rahul Gandhi's image as a pappu who hadn't achieved anything on his own.

In an address to the BJP's social media workers, its president in 2018, Amit Shah clearly defined how the party's social media juggernaut operates, stating, 'we are capable of delivering any message we want to the public, whether sweet or sour, true or fake'.[32]

Social media and the instant availability of information have not added nuance or perspective to political discourse but have taken away from it. And millennials, who consume vast amounts of news and information through digital media, have not been able to escape the perils of these systems, where falsehoods circulate at lightning speed, and marketing gimmickry is seen as far more attractive and important than facts and news. Millennials' willingness— to devour and further circulate this content, like that of many other consumers of these media—has helped sustain a divisive brand of politics where name-calling, labelling and slander have become the norm.

~

Owning the Narrative

Given the digital environment established in the new millennium, it is much easier than before, and much more important, to reach out to every voter. In January 2019, Modi sat down for an interview with Shradha Sharma, the founder of *YourStory*, a media technology company that largely covers start-ups and the new economy, and is fairly popular among urban millennials. While Modi is often criticized for not holding a single press conference since becoming prime minister, he has not shied away from giving interviews with organizations viewed as friendly to his policies.

Although the interview—which mostly comprised softball questions to which Modi responded in talking points— revealed nothing new, it was a classic Modi move: defining the narrative.[33] His responses made India sound like Singapore, a country where rapid innovation and technological progress were all taking place and giving many millions of young adults new and aspirational jobs. Responding to a question about the Fourth Industrial Revolution, the prime minister used the opportunity to not just attack his predecessors, but to also take credit for many changes that had been simply out of his control:

'India may have missed the bus during the first three industrial revolutions, but this is a bus India has not only boarded but will also drive.

These successes will not happen without the active usage of technology.

Today, India has one of the highest mobile data consumption in the world.

Today, India also has the cheapest data in the world.

Today, India is one of the biggest mobile manufacturers in the world.

Today, India has one of the biggest start-up ecosystems in the world.

Today, India is also home to the highest number of youths in the world.

Today, India is one of the largest markets in the world.'

Although some of these claims are indeed factual, they conveniently ignore how he was not particularly responsible for the demographic dividend or the fact that India is one of the largest markets in the world—it would be odd if it wasn't, given that the country has the world's second largest population. This is a prime example for how information and facts are easy to manipulate in the age of digital news and social media. Although none of his claims are egregious enough to be labelled 'fake news', the fact that he stated them as if they were his personal achievements, and that *YourStory* didn't correct that perception, exemplified the way in which Modi presents his followers with an alternative reality. Though information has been democratized to a large extent in the 21st Century, that change has come at a significant cost to accuracy and objectivity.

YourStory's audience does not attend political rallies. Therefore, Modi's messaging on the platform is aimed at urban, educated millennials and focuses on an aspirational, digital India, even as, in other places, his messaging focuses on cultural conservatism and Hindu nationalism. More importantly, Modi's professed vision for India is totally in sync with what most young Indians want: a world-class economy with cutting-edge jobs for its young. Furthermore, this generation expects political parties to be accessible. And the opposition parties have just not been present. Modi is consistently attending events, speaking at conferences, launching apps and initiatives, and making sure his message is spread widely. For instance, on 28 February 2019, the BJP organized the world's largest video conferencing call, when the prime minister interacted with more than ten million—1 crore—BJP *karykartas* and other users of his NaMo mobile application, ahead of the upcoming general elections.

He linked national progress with the BJP's electoral prospects, and said, 'Every citizen in the country right now wants to contribute in some way or the other towards India's betterment. Every Indian has an unshakable belief in himself as well as the government, and that is our biggest achievement.'[34] He then implored these party workers and volunteers to go the extra mile and explain the achievements of the government to the voters in the booths they were responsible for overseeing. The attendees on the call could also pose questions to the prime minister, either by using the NaMo app or the hashtag #MeraBoothSabseMazboot on social media.

Millennials want to be included. They want to be treated as stakeholders in something greater than themselves, and Modi understands this brilliantly. He has mastered the art of using technology and social media to communicate with the public and create an active and vocal support base to defend him and aid his re-election.

This is not to say that Opposition leaders have not been trying to increase their outreach to India's millennials. After assuming Congress presidency in December 2017, Rahul Gandhi toured college campuses, spoke at international forums, and addressed more press conferences, but as his political record shows, his efforts have failed to strike a chord with young Indians, as well as the electorate at large.

Most importantly, it has never been clear whether and why exactly Rahul Gandhi wants to become prime minister. Neither has he publicly expressed a desire to hold the office, nor has he ever made a clear argument for why voters should choose him. Most people in politics know that this kind of uncertainty rarely leads to electoral success. Voters, and young voters in particular, want a positive, proactive vision and set of priorities that excite them and get them out to the polls.

Running a negative campaign is easy. You oppose most of what the government has done or criticize what hasn't been done. But it is infinitely harder running a positive campaign outlining your strengths and qualities as a candidate, and your party's vision as a whole. For too long, the Indian political system in general, and the Congress in particular, has failed to understand this. Modi can talk the talk even though he may not always walk the walk. Gandhi, on the other hand, comes across to most millennials as a confusing, privileged and entitled individual, who doesn't even make clear promises. Most of those who might consider supporting him cannot articulate a positive reason why they might want to do so. Congress-supporting millennials sometimes talk about secularism, but more commonly, the lack of results under the Modi government. Meanwhile, millennials who are non-committal or actively support the BJP, typically point to Modi's much-touted track record in delivering economic success in Gujarat, or his flashy 'Make in India' and 'Digital India' initiatives. He has made the arduous task of governance catchy and shareable to this generation.

I found it interesting when I asked my interviewees which young leaders from any party they could see themselves supporting to lead the country. Seven out of ten times, I heard Sachin Pilot, and about four out of ten, Jyotiraditya Scindia's name came up, who has since switched parties. They're not self-made politicians or populists who rose up from the grassroots. Both were born to veteran Congress leaders, and Scindia's blue blood gives him an added advantage. But despite being similar to Rahul Gandhi in these ways, some voters viewed them favourably because they hadn't been at the receiving end of the BJP's mudslinging.

The BJP's branding of Rahul Gandhi as a 'pappu', a belittling term meant to deride him as being unserious and unqualified, has been particularly damaging. Most millennials I met called him that or used it to allude to the nature of his personality. I usually noticed this more in my interviews in north India, where millennials would often ask me, rhetorically: What has Pappu ever done, and why would I vote for him? I found this interesting because it demonstrated the power of labels. In promoting Modi as a serious leader and Gandhi as a man-child, the BJP essentially defined the latter before he could define himself.

~

Where the Wind Blows

To understand how the BJP's rhetoric and Modi's image influenced politics at the constituency level in the heat of electoral battle, I travelled to Jabalpur, Madhya Pradesh, in November 2018, a week before polling closed in the state assembly elections.

It was a warm evening when I got off the Amarkantak express from Bhopal at Jabalpur Junction. Relatives had crowded the platform, waiting for their families to arrive, and after many phone calls, I found the driver whom my host had sent to pick me up from the station.

The commute from the station to my host's house made it obvious that we were in the middle of election season. Roadside stores and stalls proudly showcased the Congress hand or the BJP lotus on flags that were hoisted above them. Three-wheeler rickshaws loaded with loudspeakers and slogan-filled banners for candidates ploughed around small lanes, loudly advertising campaign promises and imploring voters to turn out and vote for particular candidates. Campaign flyers were everywhere: on walls, windows and doors, strewn on roads, and even floating on the Narmada river. No place or person was immune from the incredible excitement of the election, and it seemed like the entire town was celebrating a wedding.

These elections were consequential: the BJP had been in power for fifteen consecutive years, with its chief minister, Shivraj Singh Chauhan in office for thirteen. Chauhan is commonly called mamaji by voters because of numerous schemes to empower girls and women, since a mamaji in the Hindu family unit is viewed as a generous benefactor of his sister and her children. Mamaji was trying to achieve something no other Madhya Pradesh Chief Minister had done before: lead his party to a fourth consecutive majority and maintain its grip on the Chief Minister's Office.

Any political observer knows backlash to incumbency is inevitable. Whether it's after five, ten, or fifteen years, at some point voters are going to demand change. And the signs of impending change in Madhya Pradesh were all there. An acute crisis in the countryside, where farmers had produced record-breaking crop yields, but suffered after crop prices plummeted to record lows. *Kisano ka aakrosh*—farmers' wrath—was how some farmers described their plight. Tensions reached a tipping point in June 2017 when state police opened fire on a farmers' protest, killing six. It seemed like things had truly hit rock bottom. Job creation was almost non-existent. According to a state economic survey I referenced earlier as well, educated unemployed individuals in the state increased from 79.6 per cent in 2015 to 85.7 per cent by the end of 2016.[35] Official figures reported at the time found that 14.1 lakh (1.4 million) youth across the state were registered as unemployed, but I suspect those numbers were just the tip of a much larger iceberg.[36] As the media swarmed all corners of Madhya Pradesh in the run-up to the elections, journalist Sagarika Ghose made a particularly interesting observation about Indore, the state's largest city and business capital, writing, 'no sharp-suited new executives are seen, no MNCs stretching on city outskirts, only rows of street-corner vendors selling the ubiquitous pakora and *bhajiya*, street foods of which Indore is justifiably proud. But should today's youth aspire only to be pakora sellers?'[37]

Matters had been made worse by a series of high-profile rapes and crimes against women and even young girls, which only added to the sense of lawlessness in the state. These tragedies had created a fertile ground for a change in government, so I decided to spend some time on the ground and investigate things myself.

The campaign had been viciously contested. With numerous high-profile personalities in its state leadership, the Congress party had not projected a chief-ministerial candidate, instead choosing to bank on the popularity of the forty-seven-year-old parliamentarian Jyotiraditya Scindia, a member of Gwalior's erstwhile Scindia royal family, and seventy-two-year old Kamal Nath, a wealthy industrialist and nine-time member of Indian Parliament. Scindia and Nath were the only two Congress parliamentarians who held on to their seats in the 2014 Modi wave when the BJP swept 27 of the state's 29 Lok Sabha constituencies. Both were born into lives of wealth and privilege. Both studied at the Doon School, an all-boys prestigious boarding school in Dehradun, seen as India's Eton, which educates many of the country's business and social elite. For these very reasons, I was fascinated by their immense popularity in Madhya Pradesh, a majority-rural and agrarian state. Neither of them had life stories which voters could relate with but were loved by many in the state. I had to go to Madhya Pradesh to investigate what was going on.

I had chosen to visit Jabalpur because its urban and exurban constituencies were some of the most hotly contested in the state. With a total of eight seats (four urban and four rural) on the line, it was a perfect microcosm through which to understand people's attitudes before voting began. The city was among the more prosperous in the state. I had heard from my father, who had spent a few years in Jabalpur as a child, and loved it, that it had been a melting pot of people from across India—Marwaris from Rajasthan who set up local businesses, Sikh refugees who found a safe haven after Partition, and industrial workers from Punjab and Bengal. In the 1960s, 70s and 80s, Jabalpur was one of central India's most thriving industrial cities. It was an important hub for the teak trade, with numerous processing plants and warehouses. It also had rice processing units, oil mills, and cement kilns, providing grains and raw material to the cantonment and ordnance factories built by the British in the city.

Naturally, I was excited to visit a city I had heard so much about. I was staying with the Mohans, family friends who were benefactors of several colleges and cultural institutions. They had generously given me a car, driver, and guide, and so, after breakfast the morning after I arrived, I set out into the city. Driving around, I found that it was very different from what I had pictured in my head. I had expected to see signs of thriving commerce and business, and young people at work. Instead, I saw what had become a common sight for me in many small towns— young men either engaged in petty trade, or spending their days in 'timepass',—either hanging out with friends, running odd errands for family members, or spending time on their motorcycles. Those employed were a mere fraction of the city's workforce. Many of Jabalpur's rickety factories were still operational, not visibly upgraded since when they were built. The population had boomed, but employment had not kept pace.

Prior to the 2018 elections, the Jabalpur district where the city is located, was represented by two Congress and six BJP members in the state Vidhan Sabha, or legislative assembly. Though I met and spoke to more than fifty people, I wasn't able to work out which way the wind was blowing. For every five people who said they would vote for the Congress, I met five who planned to vote for the BJP. Neither party had clear momentum on the ground, which surprised me. After being in power for fifteen years, I expected there to be a palpable anti-incumbency sentiment against mamaji. That was not the case. Voters had a range of concerns and anxieties but refused to blame the incumbent for them. It often seemed to me that the young voters I was interacting with were waiting for some sort of signal that would tell them how to vote.

Both parties were offering big incentives to millennials and young voters. The unemployment situation in the state was so dire that both the Congress and the BJP were promising young voters an unemployment allowance of several thousand rupees a month. Authorizing a new handout with the stroke of a pen is, of course, much easier than creating the conditions for meaningful job growth. But despite this lofty promise, and other offers such as marriage grants for young women, money to help landless families build homes, 'encouragement fees' for lawyers and tourist guides, and the constitution of a Yuva Aayog (commission for youth) and a Samanya Varg Aayog (general category commission), few millennials spoke about what the parties were promising in their official manifestos.[38] Either they didn't believe that the parties would fulfil these promises, or their purpose for political involvement was different.

It occurred to me that most voters were waiting to see in which direction the wind was blowing. Despite the anonymous nature of voting, they wanted to be sure to back the winning side, so that they could later try and be associated with it. This would increase their chances of accessing the spoils of power—such as political patronage, preferential access to public services, and obtaining permits for odd-jobs—which were crucial currency in small town India. Many of these voters had largely separated the idea of their electoral choices from the prevailing economic conditions and were more focused on deciphering which candidate would help them at a personal level.

I saw this in glaring evidence on my first day on the campaign trail in Jabalpur, which I spent canvassing with a BJP candidate, Harendra Singh Babbu, for the semi-urban seat of Jabalpur-West. A turbaned Sikh, Babbu had previously represented the constituency and was a natural fit for the district, which had a large number of Sikh voters who had resettled there after Partition. The contest for the seat was to be a rematch of the 2013 contest, when Babbu, the incumbent at the time, lost to Tarun Bhanot of the Congress, by a margin of less than a thousand votes. Everyone who told me about the race confidently proclaimed that Babbu's strong connect with the voters would ensure a victory. My guide and I had a tough time finding Babbu in the narrow streets of the basti where he was canvassing, so we let the loud cacophony of a wedding-style band guide us, assuming it would lead us to him.

In a few minutes, we found Babbu. Surrounded by about forty young men, who were local BJP workers and supporters, and a band of two men on *dholki*s, Babbu was busy knocking on doors asking residents to vote for him. He didn't say much to them. He would fold his hands, say *kamal ka button dabaein* (vote for the lotus), and then move on. But as my guide had described him, Babbu had a *natkhat* or mischievous personality. He was personable and easy to connect with. When I first met him and told him I was a journalist from Delhi (I often used this explanation to be taken seriously, since being a writer did not pass much muster among people in smaller towns), he gave me a big bear hug and told me to write about him in my 'magazine'. He then went on to remove a garland of flowers that someone had presented him, from his neck, which was rather sweaty after a day of canvassing, and put it on me. But more than Babbu, I was interested in the people who were with him.

Babbu was surrounded by a growing crowd of excited young men. They swarmed him as he walked around his constituency asking for votes, pasted some posters on walls, and threw extras into houses. I couldn't understand how so many people had been able to take an entire day off work to volunteer for an election campaign. It was basic work, not requiring any intellectual effort—the young men were primarily there to add strength to the campaign with their numbers. I was intrigued to know more about them.

Almost all of them had finished school, most had been to college as well, and they all lived with their parents. They believed that Babbu had the best shot at winning the seat. What stood out to me was not their support for Babbu, but their inability to articulate any reason for it. None of them could name any specific policies that Babbu stood for. None of them could tell me why they really supported him, just that they did. Later when I was talking to a few local journalists and political observers, it became a little easier to understand why they supported him: He made them feel valued. These young men were jobless and didn't have much to do. Babbu, like most other candidates across the country around which such groups of young men gathered during election campaigns, gave them a goal—to get him elected. Babbu gave them purpose. This is why thousands of young men—and it's almost always men—throng leaders at roadshows, rallies, or just ordinary canvassing.

Given that the BJP had ruled for fifteen years, the Congress was preparing to win, based on a widely perceived anti-incumbency sentiment. But it first wanted to neutralize the BJP's strongest line of attack: its repeated claim that the Congress was a party that appeased Muslims. The BJP and its allies have long used this line of attack to slam the Congress, claiming that the party is only interested in appeasing Muslims—are a core voter base for them—and it has always sought to give them preferential treatment in lawmaking. In order to dodge that specific criticism, Congress leaders in Madhya Pradesh, much to the dismay of liberal observers across the country, adopted a 'soft Hindutva' plank for its campaign.

I saw this most clearly at a rally held by Lakhan Ghanghoria, a Congress candidate vying for one of the four urban seats in Jabalpur. Ghanghoria had been in the news just a few days earlier because his brother had fired his pistol in a scuffle with BJP supporters. The brother was absconding from the police, and there was speculation that his opponent was preparing his own violent response. I thought I could get a great story at his rally and reached the venue five minutes before it began.

The jansabha was held on an open ground otherwise used for Ramlila shows, on which a large stage had been erected. It was a little after 7 p.m. A cold chill had set in, and a thick smell of diesel hung in the air. As soon as I arrived, my senses were assaulted by the bright lights and the impassioned shouting of the invited speakers. There were roughly 300 people sitting on plastic chairs at the front of the stage, which I thought would collapse at any moment given the crowd crammed onto it: an assortment of Hindu yogis, local politicians, the candidate Ghanghoria himself, and even a Muslim maulvi thrown in for good measure.

It didn't take long for the fiery speeches to begin. A Hindu priest who had apparently been dispatched by the Congress headquarters in Delhi accused the incumbent BJP government of not being sufficiently committed to Hindutva. The priest began his speech by chastising the government for its list of broken promises, the most important being its first, to build a Ram Mandir in Ayodhya. I was a little puzzled by this attack, since Ayodhya was outside Madhya Pradesh's borders, but soon realized it was an attack on the broader Modi government. The priest then castigated the government for breaking its next promise, to repeal Section 370 of the Indian Constitution, which gave special status to Jammu and Kashmir, India's only Muslim-majority state. This was seen as a high priority goal for the BJP's Hindutva base. Again, this wasn't directly related to the Madhya Pradesh elections, but it had the crowd cheering in support. Finally, sounding almost as if he was doing it out of a sense of obligation, the priest raised what I thought should have been the most pressing issue for millennials—*berozgari*, or unemployment, which the BJP again had failed to meaningfully address. He used all of this as evidence to call the BJP a party of failed promises, the 'Bharatiya Jhooti Party'.

Most political observers found this a stunning turn of events. Had the Congress symbol not been on the poster behind the podium, I would have never been able to tell that I was at a Congress rally. But more interesting to me were the reactions from the crowd. They seemed particularly excited by the calls for hardline Hindutva priorities such as the construction of the Ram Mandir and the repeal of Section 370. I stayed back after the jansabha to ask some questions. I slowly embedded myself in a huddle of young men who had come to the event. They all told me that they were unemployed, so I asked them if they felt the Congress would help them get jobs. But they were more interested in telling me about how voting for the Congress would send Modi a message—he had better get serious about building a temple and ending corruption. It was a curious mix of issues that were mentioned, but I realized that these were the issues that young people in Madhya Pradesh thought the government capable of actually addressing. The people I interacted with did not see employment as a core issue because they didn't think any politician could create the millions of jobs needed for youth in the state. So they chose to vote based on issues they believed the government should and could actually accomplish.

But leaving the event, what clarified most for me was how normalized Hindutva had become in the political arena. It was no longer an issue championed by one party. Instead, by adopting soft Hindutva, the Congress party not only demonstrated its acquiescence of the BJP's playbook, but also its acceptance that a new normal had been created in the country, and the only way to survive was by operating within it. If adopting religious nationalism was the price to pay for winning an election, the Congress would have its share.

The day after the rally, I had a long day of travel planned in Jabalpur's majority rural Panagar constituency. Sammati Saini, the local Congress candidate fielded against the incumbent BJP officeholder, Sushil Kumar Tiwari, also known as Indu Bhaiya, had invited me to join him as he canvassed for votes. There was no way I could turn down his offer. It was a hot day and we were going to hit four different villages before lunch. As I got into Saini's oppressively air-conditioned Tata Sumo, the candidate began with a diatribe against the state's leadership, telling me how bad the agricultural crisis was. From low crop prices to extortionary middlemen, I was quickly brought up to speed on nearly every issue that ailed farmers in the district.

At one of the villages, I broke away from the campaign crowd and began chatting with some other young men. They were a group of brothers, friends, and cousins, who were all involved in farm work. Their situation would likely be described by labour economists as 'disguised unemployment'. One of the men I spoke to had four brothers, out of which two worked with him on their family farm, alongside their father. The youngest brother was still a student. They owned just about an acre of land, but none of them had found work in other cities to keep themselves occupied. The man corroborated nearly everything Saini had told me—his family's income had been badly affected even though crop yields were high. But neither him, nor anyone in the village, intended to vote for Saini.

I was surprised. The agricultural crisis was in many ways a product of administrative and political mismanagement, and because none of the young people in the village had stable employment, I expected them to clamour for change. But the men I spoke to did not assume that it was the job of the government to create employment. In rural and semi-urban areas, many people view formal employment warily, because they associate it with what they see as an unstable and exploitative private sector; many also consider it beneath their honour because they believe there is a *malik-naukar*, or master-servant dynamic, between employers and employees. Milan Vaishnav, Director and Senior Fellow of the South Asia Program at the Carnegie Endowment for International Peace told me: 'When you ask voters about their elected representatives, whether its local, state, or national, what you end up hearing is that their role is not to engage in parliamentary debates, introduce legislation, or attend committee hearings, but to intervene in the administration and distribution of public benefits.'

Vaishnav, the author of *When Crime Pays*, an award-winning book on the role of crime in India's electoral politics continued: 'When you have a weak state that's not seen as an impartial arbitrator, the role of those who provide these services becomes ever more important.' It is no surprise or secret that Shivraj Chauhan was nicknamed mamaji thanks to his generous schemes. The electorate is therefore incentivized to vote for those who not just promise these benefits, but also ensure their access to the dole. And in most cases I encountered, particular individuals or groups concluded that they would be assured this access by someone who was from the same caste as them. Thus, the voters I met at that stop, who were Brahmin, planned to vote for Indu Bhaiya, because he, too, was a Brahmin. They believed that voting for Saini, a Rajput, would cut off their access to state services. 'Sainis are not one of us,' the oldest brother told me. 'Bhaiyaji is from our community and will help us when we need it,' he said.

For millions of millennials in rural and semi-urban areas, political clientelism plays an important, if not determinative, role in voting behaviour, just as it did for older generations. Local politicians, from those elected at the panchayat level to the legislative assembly, are judged by their ability to provide political favours and deliver public goods, as opposed to their economic ideology or fiscal plans. These favours include getting names included in the 'Below Poverty Line' (BPL) list in order to access grains at heavily subsidized prices, closing down alcohol shops, building streetlights and sewage lines, and occasionally, applying pressure on the local police station to help someone get out of jail. Most of these are fairly basic functions, particularly those in the domain of building simple infrastructure, which ought to have been completed decades ago. Weak state capacity and historic corruption in the government have blocked progress and ensured that the access to basic goods and services made possible by leaders is considered exceptional even today.

When they wield their influence, local MLAs can achieve a lot. From settling property or resource disputes to helping families access medical treatments at hospitals in cities, the MLA often plays the role of an elder brother or sister to voters. This has historically been the case. Voters usually pick those people with whom they feel comfortable. It is also why Sushil Kumar Tiwari is called 'Indu Bhaiya' by his constituents in Panagar. Caste, existing relationships, and patronage are therefore important determinants at the voting box in local and state elections.

Politically, most Indian millennials are not very different from other generations. Their aspirations and anxieties have not been able to escape the divisions of the caste system—apart from linguistic and geographic cleavages—chiefly because these impulses stem from their identities.

~

Collective Action Failure

The biggest challenge that millennials face politically today is that they have been clubbed together with every other generation, and are not viewed as a unique, dynamic generation that faces its own set of opportunities and challenges.

Although millennials all across the world—from the hundreds of thousands unemployed in Spain to the millions facing ethnic violence in several African countries—face a unique set of challenges, in many places, their needs have taken centre stage in the public discourse. But in India, it is rather bewildering that policymakers have not been engaging in a substantive set of conversations regarding the hopes and anxieties of this generation.

The West, and in particular, the United States, has developed a borderline obsession with millennials. While businesses try and understand how to sell products and services to them, and also retain them at the workplace, politicians are keenly focused on engaging them politically. Recognizing that millennials are economically and politically significant, companies and leaders are honing their communication and changing their policies, focusing on issues such as climate change and student debt.

In the Indian context, parties and politicians occasionally talk about some issues important to the youth. But rather than outline a proactive set of policies, they use millennials' anxieties as an electoral weapon. To take the case of the lack of blue-collar jobs, for instance, India's tiny manufacturing sector is not a result of the last seven years of Modi's time in office, but rather, the last thirty years. Despite liberalization, the country did not become a preferred investment and manufacturing destination for any industry—whether one considers the low-end apparel sector or more specialized segments, such as semi-conductors. *Why is that?* Although some believe this is because India prioritized capital-heavy industrialization instead of labour-intensive manufacturing, this is a problem that no leader from any part of the political spectrum has been able to fix. Since the 2000s, the two major political parties that have held power in the central government have offered nearly identical economic policies, largely comprising incremental reforms. And yet, when they are in Opposition, they attack the flaws of those same policies, as seen in the heated debates of the long-stalled Goods and Services Tax and expansion of the Aadhar Unique Identification Number program. This means that any serious discussion and debate on deeper questions such as unemployment and the country's failure to grow its manufacturing sector becomes needlessly political, and unable to grow into a broad, national consensus. This also makes it difficult for millennial voters to pick a party that might be better for their personal economies and leaves them making decisions based on narrower social and cultural issues.

Millennials' struggles, then, are largely ignored. One of the most important issues to millennial women, an existential issue, in fact, is that of safety, both in urban and rural areas. But the unending struggle that Indian women face is usually ignored and only brought up in the unfortunate event of violent crimes, such as rapes, after which headlines are dominated by the brutality of the crime while the media bays for blood. In the ensuing media storm, policies that could actually make cities safer for women are ignored. One of the most common problems I hear among millennial women is that they feel stifled in many north Indian cities because their families don't let them out of the house after dark. But few politicians have succeeded in making cities safer for women. Some governments have tried implementing measures they think will improve women's safety, such as prohibiting alcohol and organizing free transportation for women, but they continue to face harassment and physical attacks simply because of what they wear, what they do, and where they travel.

The American political arena has been roiled in recent months by the rise of Alexandria Ocasio Cortez, a bartender from the Bronx, New York, turned firebrand leftist politician, who, at the age of twenty-nine, felled one of the party's biggest and most powerful politicians to win a seat in the House of Representatives. She ran on an unabashed progressive platform, and even calls herself a 'Democratic Socialist', arguing for bold, new leadership on the environment, the economy, and in many ways, the fundamental way in which the US functions. Ocasio-Cortez has since become a media sensation, a darling of the progressive left, and bogeyman of the right. What Ocasio-Cortez has achieved is nothing short of remarkable. Most of the US is talking about her policies, whether they agree or disagree. Her 'Green New Deal', which was not even on the political radar when she got elected, went on to be sponsored a few months later by nearly every serious Democrat running for President. Ocasio-Cortez is taken seriously not just because of her achievements, but because in many ways, she speaks for an entire generation. While not all millennials are as liberal as her, a growing majority of American millennials tend to agree with the need for bold action on the climate and for a fairer economy in which opportunity is not limited to those with privilege. Ocasio-Cortez has been the face of a young people's movement that has shifted the entire Democratic Party and its establishment further to the left.

India does not have many such voices on the Left. Leaders such as Jignesh Mevani, Alpesh Thakor and Hardik Patel came to prominence during youth agitations in Gujarat. Some then stood for and won political office but have not since shaped or created a national conversation on youth issues. Similarly, JNU student leaders Kanhaiya Kumar and Shehla Rashid have made a mark in opposing the excesses of the Modi government, but once again, have failed to turn their social media success into political victories. Kumar, a former president of the JNU Students Union, contested on a Communist ticket from Bihar's Begusarai constituency in the 2019 general elections, attracting Bollywood celebrities and political activists from all across the country to campaign for him. He was defeated by more than 400,000 votes.

The staggered nature of elections, which leads to constant electioneering, as well as the tribalistic nature of politics, where leaders primarily appeal to caste and language groups, has put a lid on important, pan-Indian conversations. Policies are rarely discussed in terms of their potential benefits for the entire nation, but rather their effectiveness as electoral ploys. In January 2019, the BJP announced a 10 per cent reservation for seats in government educational institutions and public sector jobs to 'economically weaker' individuals in the general caste category, effectively creating a system in which a *majority* of seats would now be reserved. The move was made with a clear eye towards the upcoming general elections, where the party was afraid of losing its traditional support from upper-caste voters. And since young Indians are the primary group concerned about education and jobs, this was presumably a move directed largely at them. But it was clearly a quick-fix measure aimed at the elections instead of actual long-term progress. Millennials across the country are facing incredible anxiety because of the dearth of good quality colleges and jobs, and their fears must be addressed, but the latest reservation could be compared to putting a band-aid on a bullet wound. Instead of using its tenure to create these opportunities, the government chose to take the easy way out and increase reservations.

In other democracies, a clear division in ideologies between the Left and the Right gives voters the ability to choose policies that they think will benefit them. Whether parties promise to create prosperity by scaling back the role of the government, or unlock opportunity by expanding public education, clear political differences usually ensure that electoral rhetoric focuses on which *policies*, not *personalities* will serve the public best. The conversation then shifts to which individuals are the best fit to advance these policies, but that largely takes place after voters consolidate behind ideas they want to prioritize.

In my conversations with millennials across India, one thing stood out: They see problems in the world around them and have some ideas on how to fix them, but they don't see a political environment that will allow these ideas to become reality. The dirty nature of politics, with its backroom dealing and dynastic tendencies, not only discourages qualified people from running for office, but also leaves millions dejected with a system they have come to accept as the status quo. In such an environment, they are forced to rely on personality over policy.

~

Speak, Pray, Look

The 2018 winter state assembly elections were seen as a precursor to the 2019 general elections. The BJP lost power to the Congress in three crucial heartland states of Madhya Pradesh, Rajasthan and Chhattisgarh, and it was widely believed that it would need to recalibrate its approach to maintain its majority in the Lok Sabha in 2019.

But conventional wisdom was turned on its head. In May 2019, the BJP came back to power with an even larger majority, repeating its 25-0 streak in Rajasthan, snatching another seat from the Congress in Madhya Pradesh (and that too the one that belonged to the Maharaja of Gwalior, Jyotiraditya Scindia), maintaining its numbers in Chhattisgarh, and also achieving one of the sweetest victories of them all: defeating Rahul Gandhi from his family's bastion in Amethi. Modi's party also wiped out the Congress in a host of other states.

Through my fieldwork, I found that millennials had a big, almost pivotal, role in Modi's landslide re-election, and the BJP's seemingly unbreakable hold over the country's politics.

There are many theories to explain how the BJP improved on its 2014 performance, capturing 303 seats in Parliament on its own. The failure of Gandhi to present himself as a credible alternative, a rally-around-the-flag and nationalist bump in support for the government after the Pulwama bombing and the subsequent Balakot air strikes, and the lack of a clear campaign message from the Opposition all played a significant role.

Indian politics is going through a fundamental reordering, and millennials are leading the charge. They're fed up with the so-called 'Lutyens elite' and are replacing the old lot with leaders who speak, look and pray like them.

Millennials want leaders who *speak* like them. In my travels in Madhya Pradesh, part of the so-called 'Hindi belt', I often heard from college students that Modi's use of Hindi while speaking abroad made them proud to be Indian. These people saw short clippings of his speech in Madison Square Garden and his address to the Indian diaspora at the sold-out Wembley Arena in London, where he spoke in Hindi. The audience for each of these speeches was not restricted to the venue. Through live television, YouTube, Facebook, and most importantly, WhatsApp, millions in the Hindi heartland saw these videos of their prime minister addressing sold-out arenas in Hindi, fulfilling their need to feel like India could take its place at the global high table. They were also bombarded with photos of Modi with countless foreign leaders, often hugging them against scenic backdrops, providing further validation that India was getting its long-overdue recognition.

Although most of my respondents had never travelled abroad, they felt India was finally getting the recognition it deserved on the world stage, and that Modi was the messiah behind this. 'Everyone thought we were a poor and undeveloped country before Modi went abroad. Now they know we are a developing country,' a student at Indore's Devi Ahilya Vishwavidyalaya college told me when I was sitting with her group of friends at the canteen. I didn't quite understand the distinction since even 'undeveloped' countries are 'developing', but soon one of her friends chimed in, saying, 'We also like that he uses Hindi when abroad.' I asked them whether they realized that some Indians—from south or east India—might feel alienated by the use of Hindi since it was not their mother tongue. It took a while for them to reply. It was not something they had thought about earlier.

'Well most of India speaks Hindi, so it's fine,' the friend responded. If their affinity for Hindi attracted these young voters to Modi, it was also because they had a much more fraught relationship with English. Small town India and places like Indore are full of 'finishing schools' and spoken English centres. At these institutes, young Indians are taught to speak English, and the language is viewed less as a mode of communication than as a key to a better life.

Snigdha Poonam, a journalist and the author of *Dreamers*, a book that profiles seven Indian millennials, observes how 'English encodes class in India. It does so by sliding into the DNA of social division: income, caste, gender, religion or place of belonging'.[39] This is why many aspire to be English speakers, but also have disdain for the traditional 'Lutyens elite' who speak the language better than Hindi. English, and the mastery of it, has traditionally been restricted to the elite. And nobody better embodies that elite than the Congress party and its former president, Rahul Gandhi. In voting for Modi, millennials did not just choose a leader but tore down an exclusive system they scorned. Replacing the Lutyens elite and the silver spoon dynasts were a cabal of grassroots politicians and religious leaders.

It is apparent that millennials are key to this shift when you consider that previous generations had returned the Nehru-Gandhi dynasty to power multiple times across decades. Whether it was for the Cambridge-educated Jawaharlal Nehru or the Italian-origin Sonia Gandhi, millions across the country repeatedly voted for a Congress party led by people with whom they had almost nothing in common.

The BJP, meanwhile, never missed an opportunity to advertise Modi's origin story. They made sure that most Indians grew familiar with the prime minister's life, starting with scenes of him serving chai at his father's tea stall in Vadnagar, Gujarat. From there, the story goes, he joined the RSS, and devoted his career to its mission of transforming India into a Hindu rashtra. He rose to become the chief minister of Gujarat, and although under him the state saw horrific instances of religious violence, which many predicted would disqualify him from national office, his rise to power continued. Since he became prime minister in 2014, Modi's life has widely been promoted as a great Indian success story, one that could have only been possible in the BJP and none of its dynastic opponents.

This generation identifies most with people who speak and live like it. And the fact that the majority of India still lives in smaller cities and towns plays to the advantage of the cadre-based BJP, which has cultivated ties with local communities and developed leadership at the lowest levels of governance.

Millennials want leaders who *pray* like them. The BJP's Hindu identity is undeniably central to its appeal to millennials. Since the new millennium, the party has focused on rebranding itself; once seen as the home of the Brahmin-Bania class, it has aggressively changed course to embrace a more universal, pan-Hindu entity in rhetoric. After the 2004 elections, its base expanded to include considerable support from Dalit and Adivasi voters, and by the time of the 2009 elections, OBC voters overtook upper castes as the party's biggest voting bloc.[40] Although many of these new supporters see the party as a vehicle that can best advance their careers and interests, their support has also accelerated the normalization of Hindtuva in the country's social and political fabric. In 2017, after winning by a landslide in Uttar Pradesh's state assembly elections, the BJP installed Yogi Adityanath, a firebrand Hindu cleric and member of parliament, as chief minister. Many thought the party would pick someone with significant administrative experience to govern Uttar Pradesh, a poor and underdeveloped state of 220 million, but they were wrong. His appointment served to demonstrate the party's commitment to consolidating the Hindu vote. For the BJP, Adityanath's record—he founded an organization called the Hindu Yuva Vahini, a Hindu youth militia, and was known for his many provocative comments against Muslims—was an asset, not a liability, to his selection.[41] Although the party doesn't always call itself the political home of Hindus, it has made clear that it intends to serve as just such a home.

Similarly, BJP nominated Pragya Thakur, a Hindu sadhvi accused of being a conspirator in the 2008 Malegaon bombings, as its candidate for the Bhopal Lok Sabha constituency in the 2019 elections. After being nominated, she made a series of incendiary comments, including that it was she who had wished and brought death on Hemant Karkare, chief of the Mumbai Anti-Terror Squad and the officer responsible for her arrest.[42] He died the same year as her arrest, defending Mumbai against the terrorists who laid siege to the city during the 26/11 terror attacks. Such a record would once have either precluded her nomination or ensured her defeat, but in this case, it was seen, once again, as an asset, not a liability to her election.

The conventional wisdom was that her candidacy was a response to Digvijaya Singh's nomination by the Congress. A former Chief Minister of Madhya Pradesh, Singh had gone around calling the 26/11 attacks an 'RSS conspiracy'—even authoring a book called *26/11, RSS ki Saazish?* (26/11, an RSS Conspiracy?)—and had become known to many as the 'Muslim face of the Congress'.[43] The battle in Bhopal was between polar opposites: reportedly the most pro-Hindu candidate and allegedly the most pro-Muslim leader.

Because Bhopal, considered a BJP bastion, has a large Muslim population, many thought the former CM could cobble together a coalition to pull off victory in the city, particularly in light of Thakur's inflammatory comments. But when I spoke to Bhopal's young voters, it became clear that Singh didn't really have a chance. Although most voters choosing the BJP told me that they were electing Modi, not Thakur, many framed their choice in religious terms.

'Of course, we are going to vote for the BJP. *They* can vote for the Congress, but we must vote for Modi,' a group of young voters in line for a Tuesday afternoon screening of *Student of the Year 2* at the Rang Mahal cinema hall told me.

Muslims could vote for the Congress, but Hindus should vote for the BJP.

It was clear that elections in India were no longer about basic necessities like roti, *kapda* and *makaan*. Although many credit the BJP's toilet-building programme and its efficiency in delivering public benefits for its victory, millennials are more captivated by other aspects of the party. Almost every millennial I interviewed was impressed by the government's response to the Pulwama bombing and the return of Wing Commander Abhinandan Varthaman, whose jet had been shot down by the Pakistani air force, after which he ejected and landed in Pakistani territory.

'Abhinandan was brought back in a day. Sarabjit still hasn't come back,' a student in the group of friends I met at Devi Ahilya Vishwavidyalaya in Indore told me, while the others nodded in agreement.

While the details of Abhinandan's return have not been made public and some claim that the United States applied significant diplomatic pressure on Pakistan to return the commander, the millennials I interviewed were impressed by what they believed was the Indian government's doing. The entire country was enraged by his capture and seeing him return home unharmed was national catharsis.

Playing up the national security card, Modi and the BJP doubled down on their 2014 chowkidari theme. Ahead of the 2019 general elections, every BJP leader—from local councilors to cabinet ministers—changed their Twitter handles to add 'Chowkidar' before their names (Things took a hilarious turn when CNN called the then Foreign Minister 'Chowkidar Sushma Swaraj' assuming that was her real name).[44] In reality, it was shrewd politics: The nation was insecure after the Pulwama bombings and people wanted to be reassured that someone was protecting them. The BJP stepped in, playing the people's watchman.

In the past, the Congress had benefited from the national security vote. Indira Gandhi bifurcated Pakistan and decisively emerged victorious in the 1971 war, and in the elections that followed. That electoral win was achieved in no small part due to the highly successful war she commanded and refused to back down from, even when faced against an adversary backed by the United States and China. Similarly, despite widespread unemployment ahead of the 2019 elections, and the lack of visible upgradation in infrastructure, millennials made a conscious decision to prioritize national security and what they believed was India's improved standing on the global stage over their economic concerns.

Millennials, it appears do not vote very differently from previous generations. When I began this book project, I thought the opposite and so, whenever I asked a respondent who they would vote for, I also asked them about their parents' choice. More than 95 per cent of the time, they named the same party.

There are many possible ways to explain this. The fact that so many millennials, young and old, live at home with their parents means that family conversations have a great influence on voting behaviour. More importantly, the continuing stranglehold of caste and religion in the Indian polity ensures that voting considerations are largely based on which party will do the most for the voters' caste and religious communities. Finally, while the Indian public is very political, young Indians are not politically aware.

I found it nearly impossible to find millennials who knew about the important policy and political developments being debated in Delhi, whether it was the implementation of the GST or the roll-out of the National Register of Citizens (NRC) in India's north-eastern states. Nearly half of my respondents did not know the name of India's President.

In July 2018, I wrote an op-ed for *ThePrint* on how millennials preferred Modi's personality over his policies.[45] I detailed how countless young Indians I had met and interviewed either did not know much about his policies, nor had in fact, been negatively impacted by them. Yet they continued to support him. They did so because he embodied a 'strongman' leadership style. His self-promoted fifty-six-inch chest, and his many projected avatars— tea seller, young ascetic, bold chief minister, environment warrior, street cleaner—made him a larger than life personality. Indeed, he has completely saturated public spaces with his image. It is hard to spend a day in India without seeing his face somewhere, whether on an advertisement at a gas station, or on a billboard in a village. And millennials, like most other generations, are not immune to his charms.

~

Millennial Netas

Millennials will lead India soon. And the early signs indicate that in power, they may be very different from previous generations. The Modi style of functioning—unitary decision making, *us* versus *them* politics, and branding opponents as enemies of the state—could become the norm. Consider the case of Tejasvi Surya, a newly-minted MP from Bangalore. A millennial, Surya was only twenty-eight when he was given a BJP ticket to contest the elections from the party's safe Bangalore South seat. His reaction on learning of his nomination is one for the history books. On 25 March 2019, he took to Twitter, writing 'OMG OMG!! I can't believe this. PM of world's largest democracy & President of largest political party have reposed faith in a 28 yr old guy to represent them in a constituency as prestigious as B'lore South. This can happen only in my BJP. Only in #NewIndia of @narendramodi'.[46]

Surya, the nephew of a veteran BJP politician, developed a name for himself by working as a party volunteer and by giving hardline speeches to young audiences, labelling those who opposed Modi anti-national. In one provocative speech he posted on Twitter, he called the 2019 elections 'a test of the common Indian's patriotism and if you are with Modi you are with India, if you are not with Modi, you are anti-India, and that's it'. He has questioned the patriotism of Opposition parties, claiming that they have kept India deliberately poor because they are not patriotic enough.[47] In a series of tweets in June 2018, Surya called for the BJP to explicitly become the party for Hindus. He wrote, 'BJP must "really" become a Hindu party & not just be perceived as one.' He followed it up with, 'BJP should unapologetically be a party for Hindus. Must take concrete legislative measures to alleviate Hindu issues, not just make speeches.'[48]

The BJP ticket for Bangalore South was expected to go to the widow of Anant Kumar, who held the seat before his death, but the grapevine in Delhi suggested that the RSS leadership was impressed by Surya's Hindutva credentials and wanted more young people like him to represent the ideology and the party.[49]

Unsurprisingly, he won, and has since been actively promoting the party and the ideology on social media to audiences across the country. Surya's brand of politics is increasingly on the rise in the country today. He has claimed that he is 'committed' to Hindutva ideology. He also told *The Times of India* that he would 'strive hard to be an effective voice of the young generation of India' and would work towards further developing Bangalore as a 'global destination'.[50] Surya perhaps didn't notice the contradiction in combining hardline Hindutva beliefs with desires of globalization, but he didn't need to. He had already won the elections and is now reportedly being groomed for higher office.

Surya has embraced technology and social media, along with old-school political agitations and rallies to become a new, young, and modern face of Hindutva. His speeches are neatly packaged into shareable videos and retweetable content. Some of his most popular lines are against the Nehru-Gandhi dynasty and the old-school elitism of the Congress party. He accuses the party not just for being 'anti-Hindu' but for keeping India poor, masterfully weaving kitchen table issues with majoritarian grievances. This message is then amplified on social media, not just by the party faithful, but by millions who may not share his Hindutva beliefs, but have similar concerns about poverty and the lack of development.

In many ways, Surya *does* speak for an entire generation. Although most millennials, including those who support the BJP, are not wholly aligned with its cultural conservatism and Hindutva politics, I found in my interviews that many continue to enthusiastically support the party because they believe it is putting India on the global map. They are convinced that people like Modi and Surya will be the most effective agents of this change. As things currently stand, this new strain of politics and rhetoric in India doesn't show any signs of slowing down. Surya is from Karnataka, the only southern state where the BJP has ever formed government. The fact that his Nagpur-driven ideology has proven popular in a city as cosmopolitan as Bangalore and in a state outside the 'Hindi-belt' is a fair predictor for the direction of Indian politics at large.

Of course, the 2019 elections gave India other young MPs as well. Nusrat Jahan and Mimi Chakraborty, famous Bengali television and film stars, were elected on Trinamool Congress tickets and created a firestorm on their first day, posing in front of Parliament in regular western clothes which some fringe users on Twitter found offensive. Chandrani Murmu was twenty-five, the minimum age for Indians to get elected, when she won her Scheduled Tribe reserved seat in Odisha, making her the youngest woman in the 17th Lok Sabha. These three women share next to nothing in common with Surya, and they are as Indian as anybody else. But they are all in the Opposition. For now, their impact on policymaking and India's trajectory will be limited. Murmu, who is not an ideological warrior, has a mandate to deliver for her district, while Chakraborty and Jahan have been tasked with projecting a new, young image for the Trinamool Congress, which saw its Lok Sabha numbers reduce due to allegations of minority appeasement, corruption, and the rise of political violence in Bengal.

Surya's mandate, to sell Hindutva to millennials, is entirely different, and he is on the offensive. In making English speeches on Hindutva priorities, he is projecting himself as a young, modern face of the movement: articulate, English speaking, and social media-savvy. In the past, Hindutva politicians were largely Hindi-speaking, grassroots figures unknown to the broader public. They were uncomfortable embracing technology or speaking in English to urban audiences. The most common examples included saffron-robe-wearing politicians such as Sakshi Maharaj and Uma Bharti, dismissed even within their own parties as fringe elements. But Surya changed all of that in a single election. He is a young Indian, dresses like any young Indian, and speaks to young, aspirational India with his aggressive political and ideological vision. He isn't merely trying to capture power but sell an ideology.

And his ideology has a strong following. Surya doesn't call for explicit violence against Muslims or other minorities. But he says that in order to live in harmony in a majority-Hindu country like India, other communities should give up some of their practices for the greater good. 'There are certain compromises that one makes in the need of the social contract, respecting majority traditions at the state level,' he told the *Financial Times'* Amy Kazmin when she shadowed him on a campaign trail.[51] He was referring to his belief that Muslims should give up beef in order to maintain social harmony and possibly avert mob lynchings becoming increasingly common around the country.

During his college days, Surya was an active member of the RSS's university wing, the Akhil Bharatiya Vidyarthi Parishad (ABVP). In 2012, he led a group of students from Bangalore to West Bengal, where they joined a huge protest to demand the expulsion of illegal Bangladeshi immigrants.[52] He told

Kazmin, 'Infiltrators—illegal immigrants—must be detected, deported and deleted from whatever government rolls they have fraudulently gotten inside. It will be a very important priority of the government in the coming days.'

After his election, he made a speech in Parliament calling for the extension of the divisive NRC to Karnataka as well as the rest of India. He called illegal immigration, an issue that had not yet animated most Indians, unlike citizens in Europe and the United States, an 'internal security threat' as well a 'serious economic threat' and demanded the expansion of NRC 'to weed out these Bangladeshis'.[53] Given its overwhelming population of Muslims, 'Bangladeshis' is often used as a code term for Muslims.

Traditionally, because of the enduring reliance on caste politics and social engineering to win elections, capturing the 'youth vote' has never been a serious priority for political parties. But the BJP has slowly been changing this. Not only by promoting young leaders such as Surya, but through its messaging as well. In a viral video viewed more than 12 million times, a group of young Indians wearing the trendiest clothes in the market are seen rapping lyrics like 'my first vote to the one, one and only one who has got everything done'.[54] This sleek video, uploaded by the BJP in April 2019 mentioned old and new government programmes like Startup India, Beti Padhao, Ayushman Bharat, Swachh Bharat, rural electrification, and bullet trains, and had the refrain, 'one, one, one and only one, who's got everything done'. Modi, was of course, the 'one'.

Although many journalists, economists and experts scoffed at the video, it resonated with millions of millennials, who didn't follow the news regularly and were not fully in tune with the finer details of governance. Many take such videos at face value. Although the schemes rapped about have been critiqued widely, by mentioning them, the party essentially projected Modi as a leader dedicated to progress.

In the 2019 elections, the BJP appeared to adhere to the principal that the shorter the message, the greater its effectiveness. The party therefore adopted a four-letter message: M O D I. The hapless Opposition was left in the dust trying innumerable different caste coalitions, schemes and attack lines. None of them worked.

Moving forward, it is tempting to say that we are entering a new phase of politics in India. It appears that standing up for liberal values and multiculturalism may not be a winning political strategy, but it is also important to note that millennials are in no way defined by a single ideology or individual. At the core of their political beliefs is a desire to get things done. At the moment, Modi, aided by a meek Opposition and a friendly media, has been able to project himself as their messiah. But times can change. Successive years of low economic growth and even lower employment generation will at some point have political repercussions. Those associated with the lack of progress will need to have answers. Building temples or statues does not create the kind of development or employment young India craves.

About a decade ago, in the 2000s, many around the world saw India as the next big growth story. Indians in big cities were even more enthusiastic about their prospects. To the country's growing middle class, it seemed that reaching China's level of development and prosperity was just going to be a matter of time. The 2008 Beijing Olympics showed millions in India the sort of large-scale development China had achieved; investors, economists, and anyone who read the news was bullish about India's prospects.

Fast forward to a decade later, attaining the kind of prosperity China achieved seems like a dream even Indian millennials may never see in their lifetimes. In fact, at the time of writing this book, Bangladesh was on track to overtake India's per capita GDP according to estimates by the United Nations Conference on Trade and Development.[55] Ongoing economic malaise and severe unemployment have led millennials to look for silver-bullet solutions. And in such a climate, many are gravitating towards the allure of the 'benevolent dictator', similar to Singapore's Lee Kuan Yew. They feel that a strongman leader is all India needs for its problems to be solved. Hindus—largely in the dominant castes but even among some sections of the subaltern—have found in Modi the strongman they seek. His popularity, which draws heavily on his incorruptible image and the fact that he has no political heirs, has elevated him to an almost father-like status among millions of young Indians.

~

India's millennials crave decisive leaders who will deliver them jobs, infrastructure and a more secure and developed country. Modi projected himself to be the messiah for progress. His religion, rhetoric and style are part of his appeal, and he gives millennials a reason to be proud of being Indian. But Modi's appeal runs deeper. In tapping into existing anxieties and using religion and the language of development together as one platform, he has developed a following among the generation. Although many millennials consider the growth of Hindutva as an acceptable—or even welcome—development if the party delivers much-needed economic and employment growth, the rise of religious nationalism is unlikely to create prosperity for all. Majoritarianism not only increases the risk perception of investing in India, but also excludes large parts of the population from economic growth. Such divisions are not healthy for the survival of constitutional democracy, and do not bode well for India's ambitions of becoming a five, ten, or fifteen trillion-dollar economy. The question millennials need to ask, therefore, is whether Modi and the BJP's aggressive Hindutva will help them achieve their economic ambitions, or, in fact, impede them.

CONCLUSION

It was December 2019, and I was in the bustling port of Kozhikode, Kerala. The hot sun, under which I had sweated all morning, had disappeared behind pregnant rain clouds, ready to burst any second. I was there to escape north India's bitter cold and choking air pollution and to conduct my last set of interviews.

Kozhikode, called Calicut by its locals, plays a prominent role in Indian history and intercontinental trade. Islam began to spread its roots in India about a hundred kilometres south of here, in Kodungallur, where the first mosque in the subcontinent was built three years before the death of the Prophet. And almost 800 years later, a few kilometres to the north, Vasco Da Gama set foot on Indian shores, becoming the first of the subcontinent's eventual European colonizers.

Calicut was ruled by a Hindu king called the Zamorin during the medieval period. A port of incredible importance in world trade, merchants, traders, artisans and diplomats from far and wide came to its shores. Legend has it that the Zamorin encouraged every fisherman to raise one son as a Muslim to build easy connections with Arab traders and sail comfortably in the eastern seas.

I was walking around the Kuttichira quarter of Calicut. I was there to visit the Mishkal mosque, one of Kerala's first mosques, but it took me some time to find it.

Kuttichira is a largely Muslim neighbourhood. I had been there a few evenings earlier, crossing it quickly on my way to meet a spice trader whose family had been in the business since the 13th Century.

I was growing frustrated. I knew I had reached but couldn't see a mosque nearby. There were no domes or minarets in my line of sight. That's when I opened Google and realized I had been standing in front of it the entire time.

The Mishkal mosque didn't look anything like a mosque. Constructed in Kerala's *Thachu-Shastra* style, it was striking for the absence of the domes and minarets usually found in Islamic houses of worship. With a tiled roof and yellow-tinted turquoise blue walls, it was like no mosque I had ever seen before. Its forty-seven doors and twenty-four carved pillars were made by the same artisans who built the Zamorin's palaces. As historian Manu Pillai writes, 'The structure is set on a base of stone and steps run around the building where up to 1,000 faithful have gathered at a time for centuries and bowed to distant Mecca. Kerala, after all, had greater intercourse with Arabia than it did with even parts of India.'[1]

However, today's Mishkal mosque is not the same structure that was financed by its namesake, a Yemeni merchant who traded between China and Persia. That mosque was burnt down in 1510 by the Portuguese, who were engaged in a brutal power struggle with the Zamorin.

While the Portuguese were ransacking his capital, the ruling Zamorin was fighting elsewhere. He was furious upon his return to learn of the destruction they had unleashed. It was not he, however, but a descendent who took revenge.

In 1570, the Zamorin laid siege to a Portuguese fortress in the town of Chaliyam, completely demolishing the structure, and in a fitting act of vengeance, used its stone and wood to rebuild the Mishkal mosque.[2]

It was somewhat surreal to me that in 2019, just a few weeks after India's Supreme Court delivered its judgment on the contentious Babri Masjid demolition in Ayodhya, that I was standing at a mosque in Kerala which had been destroyed by European Christians and rebuilt by a Hindu king. But the story of Calicut's Mishkal mosque is an unlikely ode to India's pluralism.

~

I stood in front of this mosque thinking about it. Then I wondered why I was thinking about it. Finally, I had the answer. I was trying to make sense of Kerala. I had so many thoughts and couldn't pin down what struck me the most. During my time in the state, I had interviewed college students, young lawyers, budding artists and graphic designers, hoteliers, fishermen, religious scholars, technology workers visiting home from the Gulf, Bengali construction workers, and scores of unemployed youth. People of many different faiths lived in relative harmony with each other. I would see tables of young Muslim, Hindu, and Christian millennials at popular chai stalls, cafes, and restaurants, engaged in loud conversation.

Kerala offers some clues for the path forward: a generation with great diversity, but also a lot of unity. Unlike in other states, I found that religion was not a dominant factor in the heated political debates that young people had, that I listened in on. And it was common to see people of the same religious communities oppose each other politically, and vice versa. The debates I heard were not about cow slaughter and 'love jihad', but about the relative virtues of capitalism or communism.

Despite its high literacy rates, Kerala does not have vibrant employment opportunities. Most of the state's young people go to middle eastern countries, referred to as the 'the Gulf'—or, affectionately, 'the Gelf,' in the local pronunciation—looking for work. As I was consulting a Malayali journalist about my travel plans, he asked me: 'Why would you go to Kerala if you want to interview Malayali millennials?'

I was bemused. He said, 'Go to the Gulf or Bangalore instead.'

Kerala has excelled in educating its youth. However, it has failed to provide them with jobs commensurate to their talent. But here, too, Kerala is different; some of the things you'd expect to see in such a situation such as widespread discontent and brewing social anger, were totally invisible.

Things, however, have been changing for the better. As many of its native sons and daughters migrate back home, entrepreneurship is increasing, and a vibrant cultural ecosystem is fast developing. The Kochi-Muziris Biennale, India's first ever biennale of international contemporary art, has emerged as a major global cultural attraction in less than a decade since its inception, attracting artists, designers, and bohemes from around the world. Not only has it transformed Fort Kochi into a cultural powerhouse, it has also strengthened the state's tourism industry. Similarly, Kozhikode is revitalizing itself to become a hub of entrepreneurship and literature, as local architects, creatives and businessmen are pouring capital and energy into making one of the world's oldest ports a hub in the global digital economy. These entrepreneurs are tapping into the state's highly educated pool of young people to employ at their new ventures. Under the aegis of a Communist government, the state has begun opening itself to business and investment as new malls, buildings, and infrastructure are being built across the state.

Its universal literacy rate has created a highly aware citizenry which holds its government accountable for failure. Given the diversity of its population, politicians cannot rely on appealing to a singular caste group to acquire political power: they need to deliver services, and their constituents expect these services to be delivered efficiently. High-quality public services in administration, education and healthcare take precedence over caste loyalties. And although caste plays a role in the marriage market, it does not dictate friend groups or daily life the way it does in other parts of north and central India.

This is not an attempt to romanticize Kerala, nor is it a call for other states to emulate it. It is to say that what I found among Malayali millennials was a generation less divided among itself.

~

When I wrote this book, I had a set of assumptions I was excited to test. I had my own preconceived notions about millennials, which I was interested in validating. Surely they would be more socially liberal and less interested in arranged marriage? And surely I would encounter large groups of millennials discarding the caste system? After all that I had been reading in the mainstream media, I was sure I would encounter a generation of angry, young people, waiting to toss the status quo for a more equitable future. Finally, I was convinced that given the incredible growth in places like Gurgaon, Bandra, Hi-Tech City, and Whitefield, more millennials would be looking for jobs in the private sector.

But the India I saw was very different from the one I had imagined. It turns out that many of the shibboleths of the urban elites, such as millennials are more liberal are simply wrong. Many other attitudes attributed to this generation are unfounded as well. Millennials are not 'angry' or extreme. They are anxious about being left behind in an evolving global economy moving towards automation in a world with greater convergence. Young Indians in small towns and cities know exactly what's happening in New York, London and Singapore. They know how their counterparts live in these cities, and the freedoms—economic and social—they possess. Growing up, they were told it was a matter of a few years before India caught up with China's fast-growing economy. In 2021, that remains a distant dream. The stagnation of India's economy, the growing inequality in the country, the insufficient quality of education, and the continuing stranglehold of a restrictive social system, do not give hope. Millennials don't see many ladders for them to climb out of their current lives and build better futures.

In many places, these anxieties crippled Indian millennials. Ravindra, the Uber driver in Mumbai and Radhe, the snack seller in Jabalpur both had high hopes and big dreams when they were younger. Ravindra quit a job in Jordan for a better future and Radhe got a degree in civil engineering, hoping to actually use it. But they saw no way out of what life handed them. Ravindra, like many others his age, was beginning to get radicalized by what he saw on social media, while Radhe had accepted he would never be able to provide his children a life substantially better than what his parents gave him.

Although Kerala's economic climate is in many ways worse than other Indian provinces, its people are more confident. They have confidence in their government, and confidence in their communities. Its millennials have similar anxieties as those of millennials in other Indian states, but they have a sense of self-confidence.

At the very least, in Kerala, there is no simmering sense among young people that other religious or social communities are to blame for their anxieties and struggles. It reminded me of what Abraham Lincoln told his fellow Republicans in Springfield, Illinois in 1858, that 'a house divided against itself cannot stand'.

Although there are numerous factors that divide Indian millennials—class, caste, religion, and geography being the most salient ones—there are many potential unifiers, as Kerala shows us. Among these are: a sense of community that transcends religious and cultural divisions, a vibrant family life, and an engaged citizenry which demands results over rhetoric. These are all present, in varying degrees across India. To bring them to the surface would take great political vision, but the rewards would be huge and long-lasting. A millennial-first economy built through a large-scale mobilization of resources, foreign investment and political will, could still provide an opportunity for a new, better future.

Ultimately, after having camped out across 13 Indian states talking to more than 900 millennials, educators, business leaders, and policy makers, I can write with confidence that the common thread that binds this diverse generation of young Indians together is economic insecurity, which then manifests itself in second-order social and political consequences. Spending weeks on end at some of these places, I developed close relationships with those I have written about in this book. Some invited me into their homes, others followed me on Instagram. I spoke to some people for five minutes, and others, for hours. What I came away with was this: Regardless of caste, gender, religion and linguistic identity, young Indians are facing instability in their personal lives, exacerbated by a volatile world where technology is evolving rapidly, changing and challenging the fundamental nature of work, relationships, identity and life. Dependent on family networks to sustain themselves, Indian millennials are currently unstable and on the backfoot, unable to capitalize on the changes taking place in the world. This is, essentially, a vicious cycle with a limited number of ways to end it. India's millennials are defined by their diversity, talent and potential, and they currently stand at a crossroads. There are some paths that will take this generation forward, but they are hurdled by roadblocks imposed by individuals with short-term objectives, and there are other, more treacherous paths that could lead backward. For Indian millennials to move forward towards a future of prosperity and truly become the country's demographic dividend, we must urgently focus on removing the roadblocks that keep this generation on the defensive and focus on creating the conditions that will allow them to take the offensive, by enabling the growth of millions of stable, dignified jobs.

ACKNOWLEDGEMENTS

I began thinking about this book a few weeks after turning twenty-two. It took me three years to research, write, and complete, and I would never have been able to do so without the generosity of a wide range of people – from complete strangers I had never met before to my friends and family.

Travelling across small-town India on train, bus, and even boat, meeting people at crowded marketplaces and through Twitter DMs, and eating my weight in local street food was a uniquely transformational experience for me. It was adventurous, anxiety-inducing, chaotic, thrilling, and more taxing than I could have ever imagined. Yet it was more rewarding than any job or activity I often thought I could have been doing instead.

My first debt of gratitude is owed to all my interviewees. Thank you for taking the time to speak with me. Thanks for answering my questions even when they might have been too personal, raw, or close to home. I hope this book captures some of your aspirations and anxieties.

Many of my interviews would not have been possible because of local connections—old and new—who helped me plan my trips, hosted me in their homes, and provided me with much more than a bed to sleep in. Akshata Murthy and Binod Hampapur at Infosys; Brijesh Shaijal in Calicut; the Mohan family in Indore and Jabalpur; Radhika Shrivastava at the Fortune Institute of International Business; and Jalaj Sharma in Bhopal were instrumental in helping me find and talk to people I would otherwise been unable to meet.

I also owe a huge thanks to a wide variety of experts, businesspeople, policymakers, and academics who were hugely generous in sharing their time with me. Without their knowledge, this book would have been impossible to write. Santosh Desai, Sanjeev Bikhchandani, Pronab Sen, Radhicka Kapoor, Himanshu, Manu Pillai, Jaiveer Shergill, Nidheesh MK, Sanjay Kumar, Barkha Deva, Sudha Pai, Surinder Jodhka, Snigdha Poonam, Roshan Kishore, Samar Halarnkar, Namita Bhandare, Meeta Sengupta, Karan Mahajan, Harsh Pant, Rahul Verma, Manmat Singh Deo, Rama Lakshmi, Shivam Shankar Singh, and Sohini Chattopadhyay– thank you.

This book would be incomplete without many friends and family friends, who gave me their support and advice: Raghav Bikhchandani, Shreya Sethuraman, Madison Sparber, Vikram Mathur, Dipak Deva, Maneesh Kheterpal, Sanjay Agarwal, Niharika Alva, Anuja Chauhan, Nonica Datta, Bunuel PA, Latheesh Lakshman, Maneesha Panicker, Alya Sarna, Pankaj Gupta, Kanupriya Rungta, Shambhavi Sahai, Rohan Sandhu, Arpito Mukerji, Dina Rosin, Chandrika Gupta, Geoff Flugge, and Kamal Tolani.

I owe a longer debt of gratitude to: Emily Tamkin, for discussing so many of the themes and chapters in this book and contributing her sharp editing skills to help me better define my ideas; Samir Saran, for giving me my first job after graduation at ORF, where I began thinking about this project; Manisha Priyam for her numerous conversations with me, explaining

India's delicate caste balance and the way it continues to manifest itself among millennials; Milan Vaishnav, for his continued support; Varun Sivaram, for believing in this project before I believed in it myself, and giving me sustained encouragement to think bigger and aim higher; Sagarika Ghose, for her time, advice, and edits; Shivam Vij, for amplifying my insights before I had any platform, and never thinking twice about connecting me with opportunities to pursue; Barkha Dutt, for believing in my work and giving me an audience while I was desperately searching for one; Rupa Subramanya, for her friendship, advice, and help in magnifying my work; Aparna Jain, for her raw honesty and insistence on broadening the scope of my research; Priyank Mathur, for always being down to debate the implications of the themes in this book and reminding me about the urgency and importance of my work; Zak Dychtwald for his mentorship, words of advice, and for often seeing more potential in my work and insights than I recognized myself; and Priyanka Kanwar, for her incredible friendship and belief in my work.

Tarini Uppal and the team at Penguin Random House took a huge bet on a greenhorn, and I simply can't thank them enough. As a first-time author, I am immensely lucky to have landed at Penguin. Ajay Krishnan helped provide depth to this manuscript at a critical stage. Right from our first call, my agent, Shruti Debi, never held back from giving me honest feedback, and her comments helped me upgrade the quality of my work.

In many ways this book began even earlier, when I was an undergraduate at Claremont McKenna College. Without Mellissa Martinez I would not even be half the writer I am today. Thank you not only for your mentorship, but for your friendship as well. Aseema Sinha gave me my first job – as her Research Assistant – and through the course of many classes and a senior thesis project, became a trusted adviser. A huge thanks to my faculty and fellow classmates at Claremont McKenna for helping me become a better listener, thinker, and debater.

Very little of this would have been possible without the support, guidance, and encouragement of Anuradha Das Mathur, who has been my most valuable mentor. Thank you for believing in me, always giving me honest advice, and guiding me down this path. Words can't describe the support you gave me.

Finally, and most importantly, I could not be more grateful to my family for their support. I come from a large family, and leaned on many aunts, uncles, and cousins—from Hyderabad to Delhi to Seattle—for help. I could not have done this without my cousins Aamer, Anshula, Salone, and Seema, and my aunts Alka and Bani. My grandfather—who quite literally fits the description of a human encyclopedia—is my greatest inspiration in life and I can't thank him enough for inculcating in me a desire to know more about my country and the world I live in. To him and my grandmother—a trailblazer and huntress—thank you for everything. My sister believed in my project every step of the way and is my biggest cheerleader. I would not have been able to do this without her. My parents couldn't always relate to my work or my pursuits, but not once did they hesitate or waver in their support for this project, and all my other endeavors in life. I will never be able to thank them enough for their endless love, and for that I am eternally grateful.

NOTES

Introduction

1. 'Madhya Pradesh elections 2018: BJP promises 10 lakh jobs a year,' *The Hindu*, 17 Nov 2018. https://www.thehindu.com/elections/ madhya-pradesh-assembly-elections-2018/madhya-pradesh- assembly-elections-2018-bjp-releases-manifesto/article25525942. ece; 'MP Congress releases manifesto, promises gaushalas, loan waivers,' India Today, 10 Nov 2018. https://www.indiatoday.in/elections/madhya-pradesh/story/ mp-congress-releases-manifesto-promises-gaushalas-loan- waivers-1385680-2018-11-10.
2. https://www.cia.gov/the-world-factbook/countries/india.
3. Arundhati Ramanathan, 'The rise of the millennials,' *Mint*, 1 Dec 2015. https://www.livemint.com/Leisure/ZxgufEOH9saYXk5 RsmuhIP/The-rise-of-the-millennials.html.
4. Rukmini S., 'Authoritarian streak among Indians on the rise and it's helping BJP's hard right turn,' ThePrint, 16 Dec 2019. https:// theprint.in/opinion/authoritarian-streak-among-indians-on-the- rise-and-its-helping-bjps-hard-right-turn/335467/.
5. Joanna Slater, 'India's railroads had 630,000 job openings. 19 million people applied,' *Washington Post*, 4 Jan 2019.

https://www.washingtonpost.com/world/asia_pacific/indias-railroads-had-63000-job-openings-19-million-people-applied/2019/01/04/77a82e94-edb3-11e8-8b47-bd0975fd6199_story.html.

6. Craig Jeffery, *Timepass: Youth, Class and Politics of Waiting in India.* Stanford University Press, 2010.

7. Luis A. Andres, Basab Dasgupta, George Joseph, Vinoj Abraham, Maria Correia, 'Precarious Drop: Reassessing Patterns of Female Labor Force Participation in India,' World Bank Group, South Asia Region, Social Development Unit, Apr 2017. http://documents.worldbank.org/curated/en/559511491319990632/pdf/WPS8024.pdf.

8. 'Democratic advantage among millennial voters grows,' Pew Research Center, 20 Mar 2018. https://www.people-press.org/2018/03/20/1-trends-in-party-affiliation-among-demographic-groups/2_8-8/.

9. Michael Dimock, 'Defining generations: Where Millennials end and Generation Z begins,' Pew Research Center, 17 Jan 2019. https://www.pewresearch.org/fact-tank/2019/01/17/where-millennials-end-and-generation-z-begins/.

10. Nitin Pai on Twitter, quote tweeting the question: How old is the oldest millennial today? 'For India it would be: born 1935-1955 - Midnight's Children 1956-75 - Gen AIR 1976-95 - Gen DD 1996-2005 - Reform Brats 2006 - Hashtag Generation,' 26 Jun 2019. https://twitter.com/acorn/status/1143706481960685569?s=20.

11. Centre for the Study of Developing Societies, 'Attitudes, anxieties and aspirations of India's Youth: Changing Patterns. A Report' [hereainafter CSDS report], p. 4. 2017. https://lokniti.org/media/upload_files/Lokniti-CSDS%20Youth%20Report%202017.pdf.

Education

1. Amit Varma in conversation with Karthik Muralidharan, 'Fixing Indian Education,' The Seen and the Unseen podcast, 9 Aug 2020.

https://seenunseen.in/episodes/2020/8/9/episode-185-fixing-indian-education/.

2. Gretchen Rhines Cheney, Betsy Brown Ruzzi and Karthik Muralidharan, 'A Profile of the Indian Education System,' Paper prepared for the New Commission on the skills of the American Workforce, Nov 2005, National Center on Education and the Economy, 2006. https://www.ugc.ac.in/mrp/paper/MRP-MAJOR-EDUC-2013-25066-PAPER.pdf.

3. Manish Singh, 'Whatsapp reaches 400 million users in India, its biggest market,' Tech Crunch, 26 Jul 2019. https://techcrunch.com/2019/07/26/whatsapp-india-users-400-million/.

4. Geeta Anand and Suhasini Raj, 'Rumors on WhatsApp Ignite 2 Mob Attacks in India, Killing 7', *New York Times*, 25 May 2017. https://www.nytimes.com/2017/05/25/world/asia/india-vigilante-mob-violence.html.

5. 'ASER 2017: Beyond Basics, the twelfth Annual Status of Education Report', p. 2, 16 Jan 2018. http://img.asercentre.org/docs/Publications/ASER%20Reports/ASER%202017/aser2017pressreleasenationalenglishfinalrevisedjan23.pdf.

6. 'ASER 2017,' p. 2.

7. Amarnath Tewary, 'School education in Bihar has collapsed', *The Hindu*, 31 May 2017. http://www.thehindu.com/news/national/other-states/school-education-in-bihar-has-collapsed/article18683842.ece.

8. 'ASER 2017,' pp. 3-4.

9. 'Beyond Basics,' Annual Status of Education Report (Rural), 16 Jan 2018, p. 13. http://img.asercentre.org/docs/Publications/ASER%20Reports/ASER%202017/aser2017fullreportfinal.pdf.

10. Amitabha Bhattacharya, 'Let's not starve our national education policy of funds,' *Mint*, 6 Jan 2021. https://www.livemint.com/opinion/online-views/lets-not-starve-our-national-education-policy-of-funds-11609946913635.html.

11. Kritika Sharma, 'IITs, IIMs, NITs have just 3% of total students but get 50% of government funds,' ThePrint, 30 Jul 2018. https://

theprint.in/governance/iits-iims-nits-have-just-3-of-total-students-but-get-50-of-government-funds/89976/.

12. Sharma, "IITs, IIMs, NITs have just 3% of total students but get 50% of government funds.'

13. Ben Arnoldy, 'In India, the challenge of building 50,000 colleges,' *Christian Science Monitor*, 16 Jan 2012. https://www.csmonitor.com/World/Asia-South-Central/2012/0116/In-India-the-challenge-of-building-50-000-colleges.

14. Pranab Bardhan, 'A new class act,' *Indian Express*, 20 Jan 2017. https://indianexpress.com/article/opinion/columns/higher-education-in-india-is-failing-overhauling-the-system-can-salvage-it-4482520/.

15. https://www.ft.com/content/cd3622b0-6873-49b6-b361-e73f16b9919a.

16. https://www.ft.com/content/cd3622b0-6873-49b6-b361-e73f16b9919a.

17. Mihika Basu and Dipti Singh, 'Campus Cabinet: Half of Chavan's ministers involved in business of education,' *Indian Express*, 17 Oct 2014. https://indianexpress.com/article/india/politics/campus-cabinet/.

18. E. Kumar Sharma, 'Most private engineering colleges are real estate rackets,' *Business Today*, 1 May 2011. https://www.businesstoday.in/magazine/features/v.-raghunathan-on-indian-education-system/story/14723.html.

19. Bardhan, 'A new class act.'

20. Prashant K. Nanda, 'Employability of Indian graduates is rising, says survey,' *Mint*, 8 Feb 2018. https://www.livemint.com/Industry/5zHFaNtCAYO9lkeB9F8mbJ/Employability-of-fresh-graduates-is-rising-says-survey.html; India Skills Report, 2018. https://www.undp.org/content/dam/india/docs/poverty/india-skills-report-2018_undp.pdf.

21. India Skills Report, 2018.

22. https://www.aspiringminds.com/wp-content/uploads/2019/05/NER_Engineer_2019-V5, p. 5.

23. Sreeradha Basu, Prachi Verma, Saumya Bhattacharya, 'How a booming, USD7.5 billion industry is failing the economy,' *Economic Times*, 26 Jun 2019.
https://prime.economictimes.indiatimes.com/news/69950681/economy-and-policy/how-a-booming-usd7-5-billion-industry-is-failing-the-economy.

24. 'No impact of Covid, 83% attendance at CAT 2020,' *Times of India*, 30 Nov 2020. https://timesofindia.indiatimes.com/city/mumbai/no-impact-of-covid-83-attendance-at-cat-2020/articleshow/79487580.cms#:~:text=MUMBAI%3A%20Over%2083%25%20of%20the,and%20other%20non%2DIIM%20institutes.

25. Basu, Verma, Bhattacharya, 'How a booming, USD7.5 billion industry is failing the economy.'

26. K.V. Thomas, 'Madhya Pradesh Assembly Elections: Farmers' Issues Vs Religion in Hindutva Heartland,' Hindu Centre for Politics and Public Policy, 28 Nov 2018. https://www.thehinducentre.com/the-arena/current-issues/article25612274.ece.

27. Jean Drèze and Amartya Sen, *An Uncertain Glory: India and Its Contradictions*. United Kingdom: Princeton University Press, 2013, p. ix.

28. Saritha Rai, 'Indian services giant hits $1 billion mark,' *New York Times*, 14 Apr 2004.
https://www.nytimes.com/2004/04/14/business/indian-services-giant-hits-1-billion-mark.html.

29. 'Infosys celebrates a decade of the world's largest corporate education programme at its Mysore campus,' Infosys press release, 31 May 2012.
https://www.infosys.com/newsroom/press-releases/Pages/foundation-programme-mysore.aspx.

Economic Aspirations

1. Joanna Slater, 'India's railroads had 630,000 job openings. 19 million people applied,' *Washington Post*, 4 Jan 2019.

https://www.washingtonpost.com/world/asia_pacific/indias-railroads-had-63000-job-openings-19-million-people-applied/2019/01/04/77a82e94-edb3-11e8-8b47-bd0975fd6199_story.html?utm_term=.3d6e3f4eb985.

2. 'Over 93,000 candidates, including 3,700 PhD holders apply for peon job in UP,' *Economic Times*, 30 Aug 2018. https://economictimes.indiatimes.com/news/politics-and-nation/over-93000-candidates-including-3700-phd-holders-apply-for-peon-job-in-up/articleshow/65604396.cms.

3. Vinay Dalvi and Linah Baliga, 'Doctors, Lawyers, MBAs in the race to be Mumbai police constables,' *Mumbai Mirror*, 17 Apr 2018. https://mumbaimirror.indiatimes.com/mumbai/cover-story/doctors-lawyers-mbas-in-the-race-to-be-constables/articleshow/63791555.cms.

4. Dalvi and Baliga, 'Doctors, Lawyers, MBAs in the race to be Mumbai police constables.'

5. CSDS report, p. 16.

6. CSDS report, p. 100.

7. CSDS report, p. 14.

8. 'Average age for marriage in rural and urban India gone up, says govt.' *Outlook*, 18 Jul 2017.
https://www.outlookindia.com/newswire/story/average-age-for-marriage-in-rural-and-urban-india-gone-up-in-last-10-years-says-govt/972384.

9. 'Average age for marriage in rural and urban India gone up, says govt.'

10. Kritika Sharma, 'Inside India's giant IAS coaching factories: Hope, hype and big money,' ThePrint, 6 Aug 2018.
https://theprint.in/india/governance/the-inside-story-of-indias-giant-ias-coaching-factories-hope-hype-and-big-money/93703/.

11. Author's interview with Dr Manisha Priyam.

12. Goutam Das, *Jobonomics: India's Employment Crisis and What the Future Holds.* Hachette India, 20 Jan 2019.

13. Puja Mehra, *The Lost Decade (2008–2018): How India's Growth Story Devolved into Growth Without a Story.* Penguin Random House

India, 2019; Anil Padmanabhan, 'Jobless growth 2.0: NDA govt's and India's challenge', *Mint*, 4 Feb 2019. https://www.livemint. com/opinion/columns/opinion-jobless-growth-2-0-nda-govt-s-and-india-s-challenge-1549215724446.html.

14. Mahesh Vyas, 'Jobs are human capital: Quality of Indian jobs is falling, there are fewer rewards for getting an education today', *Times of India*, 10 Apr 2019.
https://timesofindia.indiatimes.com/blogs/toi-edit-page/jobs-are-human-capital-quality-of-indian-jobs-is-falling-there-are-fewer-rewards-for-getting-an-education-today/.

15. Vyas, 'Jobs are human capital.'

16. CSDS report, p. 18.

17. Ajit Ranade, 'Stagnant Manufacturing,' *Mint*, 13 Jul 2016. https://www.livemint.com/Opinion/DnfWP2niBegPzUeZuhWfuO/Stagnant-manufacturing.html.

18. '25 million applying for 90,000 railway vacancies shows we don't have enough jobs: Raghuram Rajan,' *Business Today*, 20 Dec 2018.
https://www.businesstoday.in/current/economy-politics/25-million-applying-90000-railway-vacancies-shows-we-dont-have-enough-jobs-raghuram-rajan/story/301522.html.

19. Somesh Jha, 'Unemployment rate at four-decade high of 6.1% in 2017-18: NSSO survey,' *Business Standard*, 6 Feb 2019.
https://www.business-standard.com/article/economy-policy/unemployment-rate-at-five-decade-high-of-6-1-in-2017-18-nsso-survey-119013100053_1.html.

20. Somesh Jha, 'More than half of India's working-age population out of labour force: NSSO,' *Business Standard*, 6 Feb 2019. https://www.business-standard.com/article/economy-policy/half-of-india-s-working-age-group-out-of-work-for-the-first-time-ever-nsso-119020300511_1.html.

21. Asit Ranjan Mishra, 'NSC members resign after row over NSSO employment report,' *Mint*, 30 Jan 2019. https://www.livemint.com/news/india/nsc-members-resign-after-row-over-nsso-employment-report-1548778444218.html.

22. 'Jobs data not finalised: Government after NSSO "Report",' *Economic Times*, 1 Feb 2019. https://economictimes.indiatimes.com/news/economy/policy/jobs-data-not-finalised-government-after-nsso-report/articleshow/67782769.cms.

23. 'Unemployment rate at 45-year high, confirms Labour Ministry data,' *Hindu*, 31 May 2019. https://www.thehindu.com/business/Economy/unemployment-rate-at-45-year-high-confirms-labour-ministry-data/article27379174.ece.

24. 'Zomato introduces 26-week paid parental leave for both men and women,' *Business Today*, 10 Jun 2019. https://www.businesstoday.in/current/corporate/zomato-parental-leave-policy-paid-26-week-both-men-women/story/353791.html; Rishi Iyengar, 'Indian startup Zomato gives employees 26 weeks paid parental leave and $1,000 per child,' CNN, 5 June 2019. https://edition.cnn.com/2019/06/05/business/zomato-parental-leave-india/index.html.

25. Amrit Dhillon, 'My life is spent in this car': Uber drives its Indian workers to despair,' *Guardian*, 4 Dec 2018. https://www.theguardian.com/global-development/2018/dec/04/my-life-is-spent-in-this-car-uber-drives-indian-workers-to-despair.

26. Amanda Erickson, 'India's Uber drivers went on strike today because they're making almost nothing,' *Washington Post*, 19 Mar 2018. https://www.washingtonpost.com/news/worldviews/wp/2018/03/19/indias-uber-drivers-went-on-strike-today-because-theyre-making-almost-nothing/.

27. Angana Chakrabarti, 'Do Zomato and other food delivery giants really care about their employees' lives?' News18, 17 Dec 2018. https://www.news18.com/news/buzz/do-zomato-and-other-food-delivery-giants-really-care-about-their-employees-lives-1975577.html.

28. Chakrabarti, 'Do Zomato and other food delivery giants really care about their employees' lives?'

29. Shreehari Paliath, 'Contract workers lower-paid, more insecure as companies reduce permanent hiring,' IndiaSpend, 28 Mar 2018. https://www.indiaspend.com/contract-workers-lower-paid-more-insecure-as-companies-reduce-permanent-hiring/.

30. Paliath, 'Contract workers lower-paid, more insecure as companies reduce permanent hiring.'

31. Radhicka Kapoor and P.P Krishnapriya, 'Explaining the contractualisation of India's workforce,' Indian Council for Research on International Economic Relations, Jan 2019, p. 2. http://icrier.org/pdf/Working_Paper_369.pdf.

32. State of Working India 2018, Centre for Sustainable Employment, Azim Premji University, p. 17. https://cse.azimpremjiuniversity.edu.in/wp-content/uploads/2019/02/State_of_Working_India_2018-1.pdf.

33. Author's interview with Radhicka Kapoor.

34. Craig Jeffery, *Timepass: Youth, Class and Politics of Waiting in India.* Stanford University Press, 2010, p. 1.

35. Jeffery, *Timepass,* p. 4.

36. Luis A. Andres, Basab Dasgupta, George Joseph, Vinoj Abraham and Maria Correia, 'Precarious Drop: Reassessing Patterns of Female Labor Force Participation in India,' World Bank Group, South Asia Region, Social Development Unit, Apr 2017. http://documents.worldbank.org/curated/en/559511491319990632/pdf/WPS8024.pdf.

37. N. Chandrasekaran and Roopa Purushothaman, *Bridgital Nation: Solving Technology's People Problem.* Penguin India 2019, p. 17.

38. http://hdr.undp.org/en/content/asia-pacific-human-development-report-2016, p. 6.

39. 'Millennials at work: Reshaping the workplace in financial services in Asia, PWC.' https://www.pwc.com/gx/en/financial-services/publications/assets/pwc-millennials-at-work-in-asia.pdf.

40. 'Millennials at work.'

41. Durba Ghosh, 'Even Bhavish Aggarwal's father wants to know when Ola will turn profitable,' Quartz, 23 Jan 2019. https://qz.com/

india/1530371/bhavish-aggarwal-opens-up-about-olas-journey-to-om-swami/.

42. Prashasti Arora, 'From Ludhiana to UK via Australia: How Bhavish Aggarwal drove to success,' Economic Times Online, 27 Aug 2018. https://economictimes.indiatimes.com/news/company/corporate-trends/from-ludhiana-to-uk-via-australia-how-bhavish-aggarwals-drove-to-amazing-success/articleshow/65411768.cms.

43. Arora, 'From Ludhiana to UK via Australia.'

44. 'World's largest e-scooter plant: Bhavish Aggarwal shares video, visuals of Ola Future Factory,' *Business Today*, 8 Mar 2021. https://www.businesstoday.in/sectors/auto/worlds-largest-e-scooter-plat-in-india-bhavish-aggarwal-tweets-video-visuals-of-ola-future-factory/story/433275.html and https://economictimes.indiatimes.com/tech/startups/ola-wants-to-be-the-tesla-of-low-cost-evs/articleshow/81378106.cms.

45. Paloma Ganguly, 'College dropout at 17, millionaire at 22, Ritesh Agarwal says he is in no hurry,' TECHINASIA, 7 Jun 2016. https://www.techinasia.com/ritesh-agarwal-oyo-millionaire-in-no-hurry.

46. Tom Hancock and Henny Sender, 'Softbank-backed OYO model under pressure in China,' *Financial Times*, 8 Jan 2020. https://www.ft.com/content/11199c32-2177-11ea-b8a1-584213ee7b2b\.

47. Hancock and Sender, 'Softbank-backed OYO model under pressure in China.'

48. Paloma Ganguly, 'College dropout at 17, millionaire at 22, Ritesh Agarwal says he is in no hurry.'

49. 'SIM card seller, college dropout, millionaire at 22: Boy from Naxal area scripts incredible story,' ET Online, 25 Jun 2018. https://economictimes.indiatimes.com/news/company/corporate-trends/sim-card-seller-college-dropout-millionaire-at-22-boy-from-naxal-area-scripts-incredible-story/articleshow/64678808.cms.

50. https://www.nasscom.in/system/files/secure-pdf/Indian_Start-up_Ecosystem_2018-Final_Report.pdf.

51. https://www.startupindia.gov.in/content/sih/en/international/go-to-market-guide/indian-startup-ecosystem.html#:~:text=India%20 has%20about%2050%2C000%20startups,tech%20startups%20 born%20every%20day.

52. Madhavankutty G, Shobha Mathur and Shaifali Macorya, 'India's underemployment crisis: why the jobs debate should go beyond roti, kapda, aur makaan,' ETPrime, 8 May 2019.
    https://prime.economictimes.indiatimes.com/news/69225958/economy-and-policy/indias-underemployment-crisis-why-the-jobs-debate-should-go-beyond-roti-kapda-aur-makaan.

53. CSDS report, p. 102.

Technology and Social Media

1. 'Selfie is Oxford Dictionaries' word of the year,' *The Guardian*, 19 Nov 2013.
   https://www.theguardian.com/books/2013/nov/19/selfie-word-of-the-year-oed-olinguito-twerk.

2. '"Selfie" named by Oxford Dictionaries as word of 2013,' BBC, 19 Nov 2013.
   https://www.bbc.com/news/uk-24992393.

3. '"Selfie" named by Oxford Dictionaries as word of 2013.'

4. '"Kiki Challenge" inspires 2 farmers to dance awesomely with oxen in the mud,' NPR, 7 Jan 2018.
   https://www.npr.org/sections/goatsandsoda/2018/08/07/636275232/kiki-challenge-inspires-2-farmers-to-dance-awesomely-with-oxen-in-the-mud.

5. Watch: 'YouTube hits 265 million monthly active users in India,' *Mint*, 9 Apr 2019. https://www.livemint.com/industry/media/youtube-hits-265-million-monthly-active-users-in-india-1554815017118.html.

6. https://www.ft.com/content/2841e327-12e7-4e82-95b1-5da63b6a111c.

7. Abhimanyu Kumar, 'A defiant rap', *Hindu Businessline*, 29 Jun 2018. https://www.thehindubusinessline.com/blink/watch/a-defiant-rap/article24287823.ece.
8. Sumit Samos, 'Ladai Seekh Le.' https://www.youtube.com/watch?v=qsigWJdUl6U&t=7s.
9. Samos, 'Ladai Seekh Le.'
10. Kumar, 'A defiant rap'.
11. Kumar, 'A defiant rap'.
12. Naomi Barton, 'Ministers follow hate accounts that made call to boycott Muslims a top twitter trend,' The Wire, 21 Oct 2019. Boycott campaigns: https://thewire.in/communalism/ministers-hate-accounts-twitter-follow-boycott-muslims; Soniya Agrawal, 'Customer cancels Zomato order over Muslim delivery boy, company's reply wins internet,' ThePrint, 31 Jul 2019. https://theprint.in/india/customer-cancels-zomato-order-over-muslim-delivery-boy-companys-reply-wins-internet/270512/; Harsha Kumari Singh, 'After call for rally in support of Rajasthan killer, mobile internet blocked,' NDTV, 14 Dec 2017. https://www.ndtv.com/india-news/after-online-support-for-rajasthan-killer-hate-campaign-police-action-1787666; and Tanmay Chatterjee, 'Right-wing group from Bengal offers help to family of Rajasthan man who allegedly killed migrant on camera,' *Hindustan Times*, 13 Jan 2019. https://www.hindustantimes.com/india-news/hindu-group-from-bengal-offers-help-to-family-of-rajasthan-man-accused-of-hate-crime/story-l1Q2iGBLIidAgj51xuwkuM.html.

Marriage and Social Views

1. Surinder S. Jodhka, *Caste in Contemporary India*. Routledge India, 2014, pp. 128–129.
2. Jodhka, *Caste in Contemporary India*, p. 130.
3. Yashica Dutt, *Coming Out as Dalit*. Aleph Book Company, 2019, p. 76.
4. Dutt, *Coming Out as Dalit,* p. 77.
5. CSDS report, p. 24.

6. CSDS report, p. 24.

7. In his 2001 book *Wages of Violence*, Stanford University anthropologist Thomas Blom Hansen studied the rise of Shiv Sena in Mumbai, documenting how the bonds of religion and caste were transplanted from villages and hardened in urban environments.

8. CSDS report, p. 68.

9. CSDS report, p. 24.

10. CSDS report, p. 69.

11. Elizabeth Flock, 'The War on Valentine's Day in India,' *Atlantic*, 14 Feb 2018. https://www.theatlantic.com/international/archive/2018/02/protecting-valentines-day-in-india/553244/; Basant Rath, 'Valentine's Day Vandalism and the Political Economy of Policing in India,' Wire, 12 Feb 2018. https://thewire.in/government/valentines-day-vandalism-policing-india; Swati Sharma, 'Why there's a war on Valentine's Day in India,' *Washington Post*, 12 Feb 2015. https://www.washingtonpost.com/news/worldviews/wp/2015/02/12/why-theres-a-war-on-valentines-day-in-india/.

12. Author's interview with Namita Bhandare.

13. 'Kevin murder case: All 10 convicts get double life sentence,' Manorama Online, 27 Aug 2019. https://english.manoramaonline.com/news/kerala/2019/08/27/kevin-joseph-honour-killing-case-sentence.html; Korah Abraham, 'Kevin case proves caste is a reality in Kerala: Activists welcome court judgment,' News Minute, 27 Aug 2019. https://www.thenewsminute.com/article/kevin-case-proves-caste-reality-kerala-activists-welcome-court-judgment-107919.

14. 'What are anti-Romeo squads? How do they operate? Points to know,' News18, 22 Mar 2017. https://www.news18.com/news/india/what-are-anti-romeo-squads-how-do-they-operate-points-to-know-1362855.html.

15. Sudha Pai and Sajjan Kumar, *Everyday Communalism: Riots in Contemporary Uttar Pradesh*. Oxford University Press, 2018.

16. Pai and Kumar, *Everyday Communalism*, p. 27.

17. CSDS report, p. 92.

18. CSDS report, p. 93.
19. 'The age gap in religion around the world,' p. 5, Pew Research Center, 13 Jun 2018. https://www.pewforum.org/wp-content/uploads/sites/7/2018/06/ReligiousCommitment-FULL-WEB.pdf.
20. 'The age gap in religion around the world,' p. 51.
21. CSDS report, p. 7.
22. CSDS report, p. 7.
23. Sai Ishwarbharath, 'India mints three billionaires a month: Hurun Rich List 2020,' Bloomberg Quint, 26 Feb 2020. https://www.bloombergquint.com/global-economics/india-is-now-home-to-most-billionaires-after-china-us-hurun-rich-list-2020.

Political Attitudes

1. Sanjay Kumar, 'The youth vote made a difference for the victory of the BJP,' *Research Journal Social Sciences*, Vol 22, No 2, 2014. https://www.lokniti.org/media/upload_files/PU-%20The-Youth-Vote.pdf.
2. Jyoti Mishra, 'Post-poll survey: BJP, the most preferred party of young India,' *The Hindu*, 29 May 2019. https://www.thehindu.com/elections/lok-sabha-2019/the-most-preferred-party-of-young-india/article27277454.ece.
3. Watch: 'I don't want to become PM, want to be a Chowkidar, says Narendra Modi,' *India Today*, 25 Oct 2013. https://www.indiatoday.in/india/video/narendra-modi-bjp-jhansi-rally-prime-minister-vs-chowkidar-423931-2013-10-25.
4. Dhiramohan Ray, 'Make me nation's chowkidar, says Modi,' *The Pioneer*, 12 Apr 2014. https://www.dailypioneer.com/2014/state-editions/make-me-nations-chowkidar-says-modi.html.
5. Anil Padmanabham, 'Young, first-time voters of 2014 check in,' *Mint*, 9 Sep 2013. https://www.livemint.com/Opinion/TIwYJUeroGoRMq9pjy4W2H/Young-firsttime-voters-of-2014-check-in.html.

6. 'India's urbanisation messy, hidden: World Bank,' *Indian Express*, 25 Sep 2015. https://indianexpress.com/article/business/business-others/indias-urbanisation-messy-hidden-world-bank/.
7. https://www.destinyjackson.org/blogs/articles-essays/how-did-the-obama-administration-use-social-media-to-win-the-2012-elections.
8. Himani Chandna Gurtoo, 'BJP's advertisement plan may cost a whopping Rs 5,000 cr,' *Hindustan Times*, 20 Apr 2014. https://www.hindustantimes.com/india/bjp-s-advertisement-plan-may-cost-a-whopping-rs-5-000-cr/story-y8x34eYh26xwoAxeRuaCoO.html.
9. Deepankar Basu and Kartik Misra, 'BJP's Demographic Dividend in the 2014 General Elections: An Empirical Analysis,' UMass Amherst Economics, Economics Department Working Paper Series, 2014. https://scholarworks.umass.edu/econ_workingpaper/172/.
10. Gilles Verniers, 'Everything you need to know about Lok Sabha Verdict 2014 explained in 40 charts,' Scroll, 6 Jun 2014. https://scroll.in/article/666049/everything-you-need-to-know-about-lok-sabha-verdict-2014-explained-in-40-charts.
11. Rukmini S., '2014 Lok Sabha polls will see most first-time voters,' *The Hindu*, 21 Feb 2014. https://www.thehindu.com/news/national/2014-lok-sabha-polls-will-see-most-firsttime-voters/article5710633.ece.
12. Sanjay Kumar, 'The youth vote made a difference for the victory of the BJP,' *Research Journal Social Sciences*, Vol 22, No 2, 2014. https://www.lokniti.org/media/upload_files/PU-%20The-Youth-Vote.pdf.
13. Ravish Tiwari, '90,000 per seat: Young India could swing Elections 2014,' *Indian Express*, 26 Feb 2014. https://indianexpress.com/article/india/politics/90000-per-seat-young-india-could-swing-elections-2014/.
14. Basu and Misra, 'BJP's Demographic Dividend in the 2014 General Elections: An Empirical Analysis.'
15. 'Full text: PM Modi's 2016 demonetisation speech that shocked India,' *Business Standard*, 8 Nov 2017. https://www.business-

standard.com/article/economy-policy/full-text-pm-modi-s-2016-demonetisation-speech-that-shocked-india-117110800188_1.html.

16. 'Did people die due to demonetisation? Modi govt toils to answer RTI pleas,' News18, 7 Jun 2017. https://www.news18.com/news/india/did-people-die-due-to-demonetisation-modi-govt-toils-to-answer-rti-pleas-1424845.html.

17. Sadanand Dhume, 'India's demonetization debacle,' *Wall Street Journal*, 15 Dec 2016. https://www.wsj.com/articles/indias-demonetization-debacle-1481851086.

18. Sidin Vadukut, Sadanand Dhume, A conservative's take on India, *Mint*, 17 Jul 2017. https://www.livemint.com/Sundayapp/aSghggr9ziYZZe9OD3UT3H/Sadanand-Dhume--A-conservatives-take-on-India.html.

19. Steve Forbes, 'What India has done to its money is sickening and immoral,' *Forbes*, 22 Dec 2016. https://www.forbes.com/sites/steveforbes/2016/12/22/what-india-has-done-to-its-money-is-sickening-and-immoral/#2611d3bf17f5.

20. Preethi Rao, Suraj Nair, Shruti Korada, 'Has demonetisation fostered a "Shift to Digital" for the banked poor', LEAD, Krea University. https://ifmrlead.org/has-demonetisation-fostered-a-shift-to-digital-for-the-banked-poor-2/.

21. 'Top economists are divided on demonetisation: Who said what?,' *Business Today*, 5 Dec 2016. https://www.businesstoday.in/current/economy-politics/top-economists-are-divided-on-demonetisation-who-said-what/story/241412.html.

22. 'Teary eyed Modi takes on rivals, reaches out to people on demonetisation,' *Indian Express*, 14 Nov 2016. https://indianexpress.com/article/india/india-news-india/modi-demonetisation-notes-banks-congress-opposition-pm-speech-goa4373362/.

23. Watch: 'Indians React on Surgical Strikes Conducted by Indian Army at LoC,' YouTube, 29 Sep 2016. https://www.youtube.com/watch?v=l41fsgHNri4.

24. Aurangzeb Naqshbandhi, 'Political parties firmly back Modi govt over army's surgical strikes,' *Hindustan Times*, 29 Sep 2016. https://www.hindustantimes.com/india-news/cong-aap-hail-army-s-surgical-strike-rajnath-informs-cms-oppn-leaders-about-op/story-Q37QbpgneLveuguZ8q4QeL.html.

25. Naqshbandhi, 'Political parties firmly back Modi govt over army's surgical strikes.'

26. Amrita Nayak Dutta, 'This is what Sukhwinder Singh, Kailash Kher charged for show on Surgical Strike Day,' *ThePrint*, 1 Oct 2018. https://theprint.in/governance/this-is-what-sukhwinder-singh-kailash-kher-charged-for-show-on-surgical-strike-day/127647/.

27. Pooja Choudhury, 'Alt News Analysis: Pro-BJP pages account for 70% of ad spending made public by Facebook,' AltNews, 9 Mar 2019. https://www.altnews.in/alt-news-analysis-pro-bjp-pages-account-for-70-of-ad-spending-made-public-by-facebook/; 'Former BJP data analyst on how the party wins elections and influences people,' *Caravan*, 29 Jan 2019. https://caravanmagazine.in/politics/shivam-shankar-singh-as-told-to-bjp-data.

28. Ruhi Tewari, 'Action, outcome & Modi: What BJP believes will determine impact of Pulwama on LS polls,' *ThePrint*, 15 Feb 2019. https://theprint.in/politics/action-outcome-modi-what-bjp-believes-will-determine-impact-of-pulwama-on-ls-polls/193584/.

29. 'HT Youth Survey: Corruption, terrorism biggest challenges,' *Hindustan Times*, 15 Oct 2017. https://www.hindustantimes.com/india-news/ht-youth-survey-corruption-terrorism-biggest-challenges/story-pIAif0WlcJkbUbQfI0w3CP.html.

30. Lara Seligman and Robbie Gramer, 'Amid re-election campaign, Modi takes the fight to Pakistan,' *Foreign Policy*, 27 Feb 2019. https://foreignpolicy.com/2019/02/27/india-kashmir-airstrikes-jem-battling-for-re-election-modi-takes-the-fight-to-pakistan/.

31. Mohammad Ali, 'The rise of a Hindu vigilante in the age of WhatsApp and Modi,' Wired, 14 Apr 2020. =https://www.wired.com/story/indias-frightening-descent-social-media-terror/.

32. 'Amit Shah addresses Social Media Volunteers' Meet at Kota, Rajasthan, YouTube, 23 Sep 2018. https://www.youtube.com/watch?v=1OW7AQxpf2g&feature=youtu.be.

33. Shradha Sharma, 'YourStory's exclusive interview with Prime Minister Narendra Modi,' YourStory, 25 Jan 2019. https://yourstory.com/2019/01/yourstory-shradha-sharma-exclusive-interview-narendra-modi/.

34. 'Highlights: India will stand as one, India will work as one, says PM Modi,' NDTV, 28 Feb 2019. https://www.ndtv.com/india-news/prime-minister-narendra-modi-to-address-1-crore-bjp-workers-through-video-conference-today-2000439.

35. K.V. Thomas, 'Madhya Pradesh assembly elections: Farmers' issues vs religion in Hindutva heartland,' Hindu Centre for Politics and Public Policty, 28 Nov 2018. https://www.thehinducentre.com/the-arena/current-issues/article25612274.ece.

36. Rajendra Sharma, 'MP growth slows, jobs decline & per capita up: Economic Survey,' *Times of India*, 28 Feb 2018. https://timesofindia.indiatimes.com/city/bhopal/mp-growth-slows-jobs-decline-per-capita-up-economic-survey/articleshow/63101690.cms.

37. Sagarika Ghose, 'The pakoda trap: Madhya Pradesh voters are crying for jobs, opportunities but parties are handing out sops, patronage,' *Times of India*, 4 Dec 2018. https://timesofindia.indiatimes.com/blogs/bloody-mary/the-pakoda-trap-madhya-pradesh-voters-are-crying-for-jobs-opportunities-but-parties-are-handing-out-sops-patronage/.

38. Suchandana Gupta, 'Congress focuses on farm, youth and women in MP manifesto,' *Times of India*, 10 Nov 2018. https://timesofindia.indiatimes.com/india/congress-focuses-on-farm-youth-and-women-in-mp-manifesto/articleshow/66566939.cms; 'Madhya Pradesh election: Congress tries to please all in its manifesto; sops galore for farmers, upper castes and youth,' *Firstpost*, 17 Nov 2018.

https://www.firstpost.com/politics/madhya-pradesh-assembly-election-2018-congress-tries-to-please-all-in-its-manifesto-promises-made-for-farmers-upper-castes-and-youth-5531791.html.

39. Snigdha Poonam, *Dreamers: How Young Indians Are Changing the World*. C Hurst and Co Publishers Ltd, 2018, pp. 43–44.

40. Tariq Thachil, 'Does Hindutva trump caste?' *India Today*, 25 Apr 2019. https://www.indiatoday.in/magazine/cover-story/story/20190429-does-hindutva-trump-caste-1504681-2019-04-19.

41. Rupam Jain, 'Hardline Hindu youth call the shots on streets of northern India,' Reuters, 18 Apr 2017. https://www.reuters.com/article/us-india-politics-religion-insight/hardline-hindu-youth-call-the-shots-on-streets-of-northern-india-idUSKBN17J1SO.

42. Abhiram Ghadyalpatil, 'BJP's Sadhvi Pragya Thakur sparks row over Hemant Karkare's killing,' *Mint*, 19 Apr 2019. https://www.livemint.com/news/india/bjp-s-sadhvi-pragya-thakur-sparks-row-over-hemant-karkare-s-killing-1555686177899.html.

43. Swati Chaturvedi, 'Modi-Shah's desperation shows with choice of Pragya Thakur,' NDTV, 18 Apr 2019. https://www.ndtv.com/opinion/modi-shahs-desperation-shows-with-choice-of-pragya-thakur-2024837.

44. 'RSS & 26/11: Digvijaya flags it off again, this time in Mumbai,' *Indian Express*, 28 Dec 2010. https://indianexpress.com/article/news-archive/web/rss-26-11-digvijaya-flags-it-off-again-this-time-in-mumbai/.

45. D.K. Singh, 'Sadhvi Pragya Thakur is a god-send — for Digvijaya Singh,' ThePrint, 25 April 2019. https://theprint.in/politics/sadhvi-pragya-thakur-is-a-god-send-for-digvijaya-singh/226553/.

46. 'CNN story quotes "Chowkidar Sushma Swaraj", Twitter is much amused,' Newslaundry, 2 May 2019. https://www.newslaundry.com/shorts/cnn-story-quotes-chowkidar-sushma-swaraj-twitter-is-much-amused.

47. Vivan Marwaha, 'For Indian millennials, 2019 is going to be all about Modi's personality not policy,' ThePrint, 28 Jul 2018.

https://theprint.in/opinion/for-indian-millennials-2019-is-going-to-be-all-about-modis-personality-not-policy/89629/.

48. Tejasvi Surya's Twitter thread. https://twitter.com/Tejasvi_Surya/status/1110289883887656960?s=20.

49. "'Call Me A Bigot": BJP candidate Tejasvi Surya's old tweets reveal his sexist, communal past,' Huffington Post, 27 Mar 2019. https://www.huffingtonpost.in/entry/call-me-a-bigot-tejasvi-suryas-old-tweets-reveal-his-sexist-communal-past_in_5c9b5d26e4b072a7f602378d.

50. "'Call Me A Bigot": BJP candidate Tejasvi Surya's old tweets reveal his sexist, communal past.'

51. Nagarjun Dwarakanath, 'Who is Tejasvi Surya, the 28-year-old BJP candidate from Bangalore South?' India Today, 26 Mar 2019. https://www.indiatoday.in/elections/lok-sabha-2019/story/who-is-tejasvi-surya-the-28-year-old-bjp-candidate-from-bangalore-south-1487275-2019-03-26.

52. B.V. Shivashankar, 'I am committed to Hindutva ideology: Tejasvi Surya,' Times of India, 26 May 2019. https://timesofindia.indiatimes.com/india/i-am-committed-to-hindutva-ideology-tejasvi-surya/articleshow/69509000.cms.

53. Amy Kazmin, 'How Hindu Nationalism went mainstream in Modi's India,' Financial Times, 8 May 2019. https://www.ft.com/content/4b68c89c-711c-11e9-bf5c-6eeb837566c5.

54. Kazmin, 'How Hindu Nationalism went mainstream in Modi's India.'

55. 'Tejasvi Surya wants NRC in Karnataka "due to influx of Bangladeshi immigrants",' News Minute, 11 Jul 2019. https://www.thenewsminute.com/article/tejasvi-surya-wants-nrc-karnataka-due-influx-bangladeshi-immigrants-105245.

56. Watch: 'My first vote to the one, one and only one who has got everything done,' YouTube, 8 Apr 2019. https://www.youtube.com/watch?v=313nuAAdXcc.

57. Ibrahim Hossain Ovi, 'Bangladesh per capita income to surpass India in two years,' Dhaka Tribune, 1 Jun 2018.

https://www.dhakatribune.com/business/economy/2018/06/01/
bangladesh-per-capita-income-to-surpass-india-in-two-years.

Conclusion

1. Manu Pillai, 'Mishkal Mosque: An Ode to Pluralism', Mint, 6 May
    2017.
    https://www.livemint.com/Leisure/io3gIOIpsDt2DBv8EYXuKN/
    Mishkal-Mosque-An-ode-to-pluralism.html
2. 'Zamorin,' or 'Samoothiri' was the title given to the hereditary ruler
    of the kingdom of Calicut. The ruling Zamorin in 1510, when the
    Mishkal Mosque was burned by the Portuguese, was different from
    the Zamorin in 1570, who took revenge upon the Portuguese and
    ordered the rebuilding of the destroyed mosque.

INDEX

British colonial rule, 1
Business Standard, 52, 53

C
capitalism, 53
  effects of, xv
caste
  based discrimination, 104–
    105
  and class, 107
Center for the Study in
  Developing Societies
  (CSDS), 21, xv
  percent Indians choice for
    government job, 41, 50
  study on religious youth, 130
  study on social views of
    marriage, 111–12
  support reservations for SCs
    and STs, 108
Centre for Monitoring Indian
  Economy (CMIE), 49
  survey on employment shrunk
    in India, 49
  survey on preference for
    government job, 50
Chaddha, Raghav, 109
Chakraborty, Mimi, 191
Chanakya IAS academy, 47
Chartered Accountancy (CA)
  test, 25
Chaudhary, Sudhir, 69
Chauhan, Shivraj Singh, 164
Chavan, Madhav, 18

China, one-child policy in, ix
coaching centres, in India, 25
  in Indore, 26–27
Coming Out as Dalit, 106
Common Admission Test
  (CAT), 24
Company Secretaries (CS), 25
Confederation of Indian
  Industries (CII), 21
Congress
  2014 campaign, 136
  campaign of, vii
  and economy, xiv
  government in 1996, xiii
  headquarters in, 171
Congress-mukt Bharat, 144
Cortez, Alexandria Ocasio, 178
COVID-19 pandemic
  effects on millennials, ix

D
Delhi
  job fair in, 63–65
  University, 46
demographic dividend, 17, 52, ix
demonetization, 147–50
Desai, Santosh, 96
Devi Ahilya Vishwavidyalaya
  (DAVV), 27, 186
Dhume, Sadanand, 148
Digital India, 163
District Collector, role of, 44–45
Drèze, Jean, 31
Dr Himanshu, 53